ACKNOWLEDGMENTS

M OST OF THE essays published here were presented within the past several years as part of the activities of the Old English Colloquium of the University of California, Berkeley. Both the student officers of the Colloquium and its university sponsors (including the Graduate Assembly, the Associated Students of the University of California, the Department of English, the Medieval Studies Program, and the Dean of the Graduate Division) deserve thanks for their generous support in making these events possible. In addition, thanks are due the editors of *Scandinavian Studies* for their care in producing these essays as a special issue of that journal.

Old English Colloquium
Series No. 4

ANGLO-SCANDINAVIAN ENGLAND

Norse–English Relations in the Period before the Conquest

Edited by
John D. Niles and Mark Amodio

UNIVERSITY
PRESS OF
AMERICA

Lanham • New York • London

Library of Congress Cataloging–in–Publication Data

Anglo–Scandinavian England : Norse–English relations in the period
before the Conquest / edited by John D. Niles and Mark Amodio.
p.   cm.
(Old English Colloquium series ; no. 4)
Includes bibliographies.
1. Great Britain– –History– –Anglo–Saxon period, 449–1066. 2. Great
Britain– –Foreign relations– –Scandinavia. 3. Scandinavia– –Foreign
relations– –Great Britain. 4. Northmen– –England– –History.
5. Vikings. I. Niles, John D. II. Amodio, Mark. III. Series: Old
English Colloquium series (Berkeley, Calif.) ; no. 4.
DA158.A54   1988   88–31728 CIP
942.01– –dc19

ISBN: 978-0-8191-7268-6

TABLE OF CONTENTS

INTRODUCTION: THE VIKINGS AND ENGLAND

JOHN D. NILES
MARK AMODIO
University of California, Berkeley

W HEN THE FIRST longships approached Lindisfarne in the summer of 793, the vikings found an undefended coast and a relatively fragmented society of minor kingdoms. There was no England in the modern sense. Unprepared for warfare against outsiders, the Angles and Saxons who had been working the land in relative peace for the previous three centuries were hard put to defend themselves against a determined raiding that soon gave way to the sustained threat of armies that wintered in England. By improving their military defenses as well as stiffening their backbone, the English of Wessex and southwest Mercia eventually succeeded in making a treaty whereby they would remain undisturbed in their territories, while Norse rule was to remain unchallenged in the area roughly north and east of the Thames and Watling Street.

The story of these campaigns and the treaty of 878 is written in the prose annals of the *Anglo-Saxon Chronicle*. Also told in the *Chronicle* is how Alfred's son Edward the Elder subsequently won control of eastern Mercia and East Anglia. Soon after Athelstan came to the throne in 924, all England with the exception of Northumbria was united under his rule, and Northumbria soon followed. What is omitted from the *Chronicle* is an account of the political and social accommodations by which the Anglo-Saxons and Danes arrived at this unity: that is, an account of the detailed transformations by which the separate kingdoms of the Heptarchy were first reorganized into two parts, English-ruled and Danish-ruled, and then integrated into a single kingdom, Anglo-Scandinavian England.

The use of this term will perhaps surprise those who are accustomed to the anglocentric views that find expression in some of the older histories. According to this time-honored perspective, the viking raids and incursions were a temporary aberration, an attack on English people and institutions (particularly the Church) by pagans whose ferocity was eventually turned aside. As John Richard Green put it in his standard *Short History of the English People*, "When the wild burst of the storm was over, land, people, government, reappeared unchanged" (2nd ed., New

York: American Book Co. [1900], 87). This view, which owes much to the patriotic prose of the *Chronicle*, ignores the restructuring of English society and culture that resulted from the Norse settlements. Edward's string of military victories is sometimes spoken of as a "reconquest" of the Danelaw, as if the Danelaw had been his to regain. Instead, the stimulus of the viking incursions encouraged the development of a new kind of government in England, a centralized monarchy based in part on the Carolingian model.

The first seven rulers of this kingdom, from Athelstan (924–39) to Ethelred (978–1016), were of the West Saxon royal line. The next two, Swein Forkbeard (1013–14) and Cnut the Great (1016–35), were Danes. England under Cnut enjoyed the benefits of stable and enlightened leadership and for a time became part of a small empire that spanned the North Sea, encompassing Norway, Scotland, and parts of Sweden as well as Denmark. That loose political unity disintegrated soon after Cnut's death, and within a few years the West Saxon royal line reasserted itself in the person of Edward the Confessor (1042–66). If, upon Edward's death, Harold Hardradi had been successful in his attempt to win the English throne, a new alliance of English and Norsemen would have emerged with long-term effects that could have proven momentous. As things turned out, Harold's defeat and death at Stamford Bridge, coupled with the equally decisive Norman victory at Hastings three weeks later, signaled the end of England's close relations with Scandinavia. Following William the Bastard's victory at Hastings, a new and highly disciplined set of invaders, some of them of Norse stock, imposed their authority on Britain and made it more firmly part of the Continent than it had been since Roman times. Although the North Sea trade routes remained open, interconnections with France assumed far greater importance. From the late eleventh century onward, most people of Norse descent in England have pursued the business of life without intercommunication with Scandinavia.

The lasting effects of Norse settlement in Britain have yet to be fully assessed. Scandinavian influence on shipbuilding and stockbreeding is manifest; influence on crop cultivation is less so. Norsemen were instrumental in building up overseas trade as well as towns that throve on trade, notably, York and the five boroughs of Lincoln, Nottingham, Derby, Leicester, and Stamford. Danish law left a strong mark on the development of English legal and administrative institutions during the tenth and eleventh centuries, but that influence was partly annulled by the coming of the Normans. Place-names (particularly village names ending in *-thorpe* or *-by*) give an indication of the density and limits of Norse settlement in the northern shires and the East Midlands. Norse influence on the dialects of these regions is still manifest. The vikings' predilection for taking loot where they could get it is evident in such borrowings into the standard tongue as *crave, get, ransack, rive, scare, take,* and *thrust*. Also from Old Norse, however, come *give* (in the modern pronunciation) and *gift* (in the modern pronunciation and sense). Norse borrowings extend so pervasively into common English speech, even including bedrock forms in the pronoun and verb systems, as to indicate a long symbiosis of two peoples of similar status and culture.

The papers of the present volume are intended to contribute to a more precise assessment of the interconnections between England and Scandinavia during the period from the establishment of the Danelaw to the Norman Conquest. The essays fall into three groups concerned with history, myth, and the language of poetry.

Theodore Andersson's essay advances the hypothesis that, despite the bad press Ethelred "the Unready" has suffered in English histories beginning with the *Chronicle*, Ethelred countered the renewed viking attacks of the early part of his reign with a coherent plan. According to a settlement that he seems to have struck with Olaf Tryggvason, Olaf was to restrict his viking activities to Norway, where Ethelred would materially support him in his efforts to gain the throne. Olaf, on his side, would adopt the Christian faith and would promulgate it among his people, to the advancement of peaceful relations with the English. Ethelred's aim was to nullify what was clearly a significant Norse threat to his realm. That in the end he failed, in the face of renewed assaults from Denmark, is a statement less about his competence than about Swein's and Cnut's rising strength.

In a short reply to Andersson, Phyllis Brown points out that Ethelred's policy, if he indeed had one, was undercut by inept decisions and by weakness or disloyalty on the part of those who were supposed to enact it.

In a more detailed treatment of relations between Ethelred, Olaf Tryggvason, and Swein Forkbeard, Peter Sawyer acknowledges the need to rehabilitate Ethelred's reputation. Still he doubts that any treaty signed by Ethelred and Olaf in 994 had a dramatic impact on the way that Anglo-Norse relations were unfolding. Olaf was only one of a number of powerful vikings of the day. His conversion to the Christian faith was no guarantee of pacific intentions. If Ethelred hoped to secure his borders by treating with Olaf, those hopes were soon dashed by Olaf's death at the hands of Swein.

The articles by John Lindow and John McKinnell respond to the argument that important elements of Norse mythology were shaped by the vikings' contact with English Christianity in the Danelaw. Lindow reviews the textual evidence that has been thought to support this assertion and finds it wanting, as it is based on broadly Christian parallels rather than specifically English ones. He shows reason to doubt that Wulfstan's homilies influenced the phrasing of *Vǫluspá*. Instead, he suggests that, given the omnipresence of basic Christian ideas and modes of expression in Europe during the time before *Vǫluspá* was written down, it is futile to look for specific models operating on a given turf.

McKinnell seconds this conclusion and backs it with further textual arguments and evidence from Northumbrian sculpture, particularly the carved stones from Gosforth Church in Cumbria. Although composition of Vǫluspá somewhere in the Danelaw cannot be ruled out, the evidence of the sculptures does not confirm that a mythological work of this character would have emerged from that locale. Incidentally, McKinnell points out that some Northumbrian sculpture on pagan themes was used to reinforce the superiority of the Christian faith.

Roberta Frank disputes the accepted notion that skaldic verse had little influence on Old English poetic style. She first shows that a sequence of fanciful metaphors in the Old English poetic paraphrase of Exodus is based on traditional Norse shield-kennings. An audience accustomed to skaldic diction would have had no difficulty interpreting the sequence and may have enjoyed the poet's virtuosity. Frank also suggests that even though *Beowulf* is free of obvious skaldicisms, several of its features point to Northern influence. Likewise, the common Old English motif of the carrion birds and beasts of battle, particularly as presented in *Exodus*, may derive from skaldic models rather than being an old Germanic inheritance.

Frank's essay should stimulate a more careful evaluation of Anglo-Norse literary relations in the period after the Scandinavian settlements. To judge from both fictionalized accounts in the sagas and the direct evidence of skaldic poems that are based on events in British history, many skalds practiced their art in the British Isles. A tongue that was influencing English speech in myriad ways must have had an effect on the special language of Old English poetry as well. That effect was less pronounced because of the naturally conservative nature of the literary tradition. In addition, Norse influence on English poetry was curtailed by the general collapse of vernacular letters in England as a result of the Conquest. In a note that supplements Frank's article, John Niles accounts for several features of the *Battle of Brunanburh* by reference to the language and art of the skalds.

The last item in this collection, "Maldon As It Really Was," came into the editors' hands anonymously. The manuscript of which it is a transcription was discovered some years ago after having fallen behind the stacks in Widener Library. Unfortunately, the manuscript seems to have suffered a similar fate again, and thus we are unable to verify the authenticity of the particular linguistic forms given here. As the piece may have interest for its bearing on events of the year 991, not to mention larger literary and historical issues, we print it as received.

The present volume contributes to a small forest of recent publications in the field of Anglo-Norse studies. Many of these are cited in the notes to individual articles. It is worth remarking that the current revival of interest in Viking Age culture in the British Isles has been stimulated by museum exhibits, including the splendid collection of viking artifacts that was displayed at the British Museum and the Metropolitan Museum of

Art in New York in 1980. The relation of the Sutton Hoo ship burial to early boat graves from Sweden was brought out through an exhibit in the Historical Museum in Stockholm that same year. Excavations at the Coppergate in York continue to lead to the display of objects illustrating the conditions of life in what was once a thriving Anglo-Norse town, Jorvík. The many people who have helped organize these exhibits deserve thanks for making the interconnections between medieval England and Scandinavia more visible to our eyes.

THE VIKING POLICY OF ETHELRED THE UNREADY

THEODORE M. ANDERSSON

Stanford University

IN THE YEAR 994 King Ethelred the Unready invited, or summoned, the viking chieftain Olaf Tryggvason to a parley at Andover. This parley was occasioned by the first phase of the dire events that brought about a hiatus in the Anglo-Saxon dynasty, paved the way for Danish rule during a period of twenty-six years, and burdened Ethelred with his spiteful nickname. The meeting at Andover and the occurrences that precipitated it are reported in good detail by the *Anglo-Saxon Chronicle* for 994. Dorothy Whitelock's translation of the entry (version C) runs as follows:

> In this year Olaf and Swein came to London on the Nativity of St. Mary with 94 ships, and they proceeded to attack the city stoutly and wished also to set it on fire; but there they suffered more harm and injury than they ever thought any citizens would do to them. But the holy Mother of God showed her mercy to the citizens on that day and saved them from their enemies. And these went away from there, and did the greatest damage that ever any army could do, by burning, ravaging, and slaying, everywhere along the coast, and in Essex, Kent, Sussex, and Hampshire; and finally they seized horses and rode as widely as they wished, and continued to do indescribable damage. Then the king and his councillors determined to send to them and promise them tribute and provisions, on condition that they should cease that harrying. And they then accepted that, and the whole army came then to Southampton and took winter quarters there; and they were provisioned throughout all the West Saxon kingdom, and they were paid 16,000 pounds in money.
>
> Then the king sent Bishop Ælfheah and Ealdorman Æthelweard for King Olaf, and hostages were given to the ships meanwhile. And they then brought Olaf to the king at Andover with much ceremony, and King Ethelred stood sponsor to him at confirmation, and bestowed gifts on him royally. And then Olaf promised—as also he performed—that he would never come back to England in hostility [Whitelock 235–36].

We learn from the entry that Olaf attacked England in force, as he had done once before in 991, but was persuaded by Ethelred to desist from further attacks. Olaf was as good as his word and disappears from the *Chronicle* and from English history at that moment. Thereafter he appears only in Norse literature, where he has been the subject of three separate biographies as well as a figure in five general histories and many sagas (Lönnroth; Halldórsson 1967). We know from these sources that the year after his meeting with Ethelred at Andover he returned to his native Norway, from which he had fled as a child; overthrew the reigning heathen monarch, Hákon jarl; had himself proclaimed king; and set about the work of converting Norway to Christianity. The five short years of his mission from 995 to 1000 were astonishingly successful; he converted not only Norway but the Orkney Islands, Iceland, and Greenland as well.

Olaf's swift success is something of a historical mystery. How was this adventurer, who had spent all of his adult life outside of Norway, who had no power base and no tax base, able to impose his will both politically and religiously on his native country and her outlying dependencies with such rapidity? Whether or not there was a long period of preliminary missionary work (Birkeli 1971), the *Anglo-Saxon Chronicle* for 994 provides a possible key to Olaf's meteoric rise. There may have been some hidden agendum at Andover when he met with King Ethelred, some calculated connection between his disappearance from English history and his grand entry into Norwegian history. The English may well have indicated to Olaf that Norway would be a better field for his warlike endeavors. They could have declared themselves ready to assist if only Olaf would divert his energies to another coast. We are told that they gave him gifts; such gifts could have included arms, supplies, or even ships. The English may have suggested further that their assistance would be facilitated by Olaf's reaffirmation of his Christian sympathies—hence his confirmation with Ethelred as sponsor. We can in any event be quite certain that the English provided him with clergy for the conversion of Norway, because this clergy is mentioned in the earliest Scandinavian sources (Ellehøj 256–57). In other words, Olaf Tryggvason's success would be easier to understand if we assume that he was abetted by an English ally.

Collaboration from across the North Sea would be readily comprehensible in terms of an English foreign policy designed to neutralize the Norwegian vikings by converting them to religious like-mindedness and calculated to drive a wedge between Norwegians and Danes, thus dividing the attackers. This policy could capitalize on a history of hostility between Norway and Denmark in the tenth century, a history that extended well into the eleventh century. It is easy to imagine, at this remove in time, that the vikings presented a solid front against their victims, but the internal splits in the viking camp were complex, and warfare between Danes and Norwegians was endemic.

It might be argued that such a clear English policy is unlikely because it must be attributed to the least reputable of all English kings, Ethelred the Unready, who reigned throughout the period in question, from 978 to 1016. His very name belies the formulation of policy inasmuch as the Old English original of "Unready," *unræd,* seems to mean "bad policy" or perhaps "no policy at all" (Keynes 1978, p. 240 and note 77). Most injurious to Ethelred's reputation is the lavish scale on which he paid off the Danes: 10,000 pounds in 991, 16,000 pounds in 994, 24,000 pounds in 1002, 36,000 pounds in 1007, 48,000 pounds in 1012, and 80,000 pounds paid to King Cnut's army—for a grand total of 214,000 pounds in twenty-five years (John 174). As a result of this apparent giveaway, Ethelred has acquired an unenviable position in the folklore of history as a figure of fun and a byword for futile appeasement (Keynes 1978, pp. 250 and 252, notes 65 and 88). Rudyard Kipling so stamped him in a poem entitled "Danegeld (A.D. 980–1016)," reprinted in the standard edition of his works (716–17), and as recently as 1977 a collection of humorous verse included a mini-ballad opposite a picture of Ethelred sound asleep in bed (Logue and Kitchen, under the letter U). The refrain runs:

> Ethelred! Ethelred!
> Spent his royal life in bed,
> One shoe off and one shoe on,
> Greatly loved by everyone.

Ethelred as slugabed might easily be taken as modern malice, but the image derives from no less a medieval authority than William of Malmesbury:

> Rex interea strenuus et pulchre ad dormiendum factus, tanta negotia postponens, oscitabat; et si quando resipuerat ut vel cubito se attolleret, confestim, vel gravante desidia, vel adversante fortuna, in miserias recidebat.

> (In the meantime, the king, adept and well fitted for sleep, put off such great matters and yawned; and if ever he recovered to the point of rising from his bed, he was immediately overcome by inertia or adverse fortune and relapsed into his miserable state
> [Keynes 1978, p. 238, note 55].)

Without detailing the theme of Ethelred's indolence in later historiography, we may content ourselves with the assessment of the great German legal scholar of the nineteenth century, Konrad Maurer, who dismissed Ethelred monosyllabically as "faul und feig" (466), thus adding the insult of alliteration to the injury of a poor opinion.

The lampoon of 1977 may well mark the absolute nadir of Ethelred's historical fortunes, for in the same year the first sign of rehabilitation appeared. Eric John published a paper in which he pointedly omitted the damaging nickname and referred to the king throughout as Æthelred II. He reminded us that the payment of Danegeld was as old as Alfred the Great and showed that Ethelred inherited his troubles from the promonastic policy of his father, Edgar; the transfer of estates from secular to ecclesiastical lords; and the ensuing political unrest. The viking invasions were therefore exacerbated, as he says, by "what amounted to an endemic civil war" (183). On the positive side, John notes that Ethelred successfully exerted pressure on Normandy to close its harbors to viking fleets (189). A letter from Pope John XV suggests that the pressure began as early as 990, and Ethelred's diplomacy culminated when he married the Norman princess Emma in 1002 (Fauroux 22). John concludes that Ethelred "tried with some success to divide his enemies" (191). The larger point is that if he pursued a policy of dividing Danes and Normans, it is not unreasonable to suppose that he may also have pursued a policy of dividing Danes and Norwegians.

A year after the appearance of Eric John's paper the thousandth anniversary of Ethelred's succession to the throne was marked by the publication of Hill's volume of millenary papers. This volume goes a long way toward balancing our view of Ethelred. In the contribution already cited Simon Keynes traces the decline of Ethelred's reputation and argues that our historical perception is determined by the retrospective nature of our sources, all of which, including the relevant sections of the *Anglo-Saxon Chronicle,* were written after the fact and were colored by the final English failure and the Danish triumph. These sources tended to convert the reality of a long seesaw struggle into a tale of foregone woe.

Other papers in the millenary collection are no less revealing. Pauline Stafford shows that there is evidence of growing royal strength in the 990s, a reduction of the ealdormanries and their replacement by smaller units under the control of reeves—that is, a diffusion of noble prerogatives in favor of central control—an increased number of grants of privilege in lieu of outright donations of land, and a widening sphere of grant activity attributable to extended royal power (Stafford). In a thorough reassessment of Ethelred's laws, previously thought to be jumbled and rhetorically inflated, Patrick Wormald argues that much of the blame for that reputation can be laid at the doorstep of Archbishop Wulfstan, who rewrote the laws "along the lines of Carolingian pastoral imperialism" (77). With this layer stripped away Ethelred's record is no better or worse than what went before and after; his reign is part of a steady continuity. Wormald concludes, "Æthelred was no Justinian, no Charlemagne, no Æthelstan even. But his *ge-raed-nessa* ('decrees') supply no justification for the immortal and malicious pun, Aeþel-raed Un-raed" (77).

In a study of heriot (*heregeatu*), that is, the repayment of the tenant's arms to the lord upon the tenant's death, Nicholas P. Brooks concludes from a survey of wills written during Ethelred's reign that the king increased the imposition of armaments and provided for a larger number of armed men: "Henceforth his followers were to have men with the full complement of weapons and body-armour, to have relief horses and lightly-armed attendants" (90). From this observation it seems clear to Brooks that Ethelred was alive to military realities. In yet another area of public endeavor Richard Gem's survey of the building program under Ethelred shows that there is no suggestion of a reduction until 1005, when economic resources were presumably shifted to contend with the viking attacks that characterized the last years of his reign.

Most suggestive of all perhaps is the numismatic evidence. In separate papers Michael Dolley and D. M. Metcalf develop their earlier analysis of Ethelred's coinage in terms of a regularly scheduled sequence of issues at six-year intervals. Dolley argues that in this area, too, there is strong evidence of central planning and continuity. He notes in particular that even in the second decade of the eleventh century, during and after Ethelred's downfall, we have thousands of pennies struck at Ethelred's seventy-nine mints, but not a single penny bearing the name of the Danish conqueror Swein Forkbeard (129). When King Cnut assumed control, he also adhered to Ethelred's system. Dolley concludes, "The numismatist for one recognizes in Æthelræd (or perhaps in those he allowed to guide him) an organizational ability of a very high order" (130).

Metcalf's statistics point in the same direction. He calculates the production of coin at Ethelred's mints and the probable percentage of drain on English currency occasioned by the repeated payment of geld. This drain was indeed formidable, perhaps as high as seventy percent of native currency in the late "helmet" series of coins. But such a crushing impost requires an explanation, and Metcalf offers one. He points out that the Scandinavian coin finds of this period contain nearly twice as many continental coins as English coins (180). These continental coins came largely from England's trading partners in the Netherlands and Rhineland; they suggest that there may also have been a very significant flow of continental currency into England, that is, a large balance of payments surplus. Metcalf concludes, "Subject to the results of more detailed numismatic studies, then, there is strong reason to suspect that in the 990s money may have flowed into England as payment for exports even faster than the Danish host could siphon it off" (180). This hypothesis opens the interesting possibility that Ethelred could actually afford the infamous Danegelds that are the chief source of his disrepute.

A further readjustment in our perception of King Ethelred occurred two years after the appearance of the millenary papers when Simon Keynes published a study of Ethelred's diplomas. Keynes proposes a tripartite division of Ethelred's reign rather different from the tripartite scheme advocated by William of Malmesbury in the twelfth century. According to William, Ethelred's reign was cruel in the beginning (because of his supposed murder of his half brother Edward), wretched in the middle, and disgraceful at the end. Keynes suggests rather that it was beyond his control in the beginning, well conducted in the middle, and admittedly out of hand at the end (Keynes 1980, 231). The charge of cruelty growing out of Edward's murder is almost surely unjustified, if for no other reason than because Ethelred was only about nine years old at the time (164). In the middle period Keynes finds evidence of a well-organized royal chancery and an administration in which the king surrounded himself with competent advisers (189). The end of his reign was certainly a disaster as England crumbled before successive onslaughts of armies numbering as many as ten thousand men and led by Thorkell the Tall, Swein Forkbeard, and King Cnut. But it should be remembered that Ethelred held on doggedly until the end. As late as 1013 his diplomacy succeeded in detaching Thorkell the Tall from the Danish force. In 1014 he fled to Normandy, but he was recalled and returned to England at the beginning of 1016. His death shortly thereafter prevents us from knowing whether there was any further resilience in his reign.

An area that has not, to my knowledge, been explored with the same thoroughness as Ethelred's diplomas, coinage, and laws is his foreign policy, but there are indications that he was no less active in that arena. We know from the papal letter of 991 that Ethelred concluded a treaty in that year with Duke Richard of Normandy, a treaty apparently designed to inhibit viking operations based in Norman harbors. The year 991 is, however, more famous as the date of the Battle of Maldon and the date of the first great Danegeld in the amount of ten thousand pounds. That date has been taken as a turning point for the worse in English morale. Eric John wrote, "Up to 991 and the defeat of Maldon the English, it seems to me, expected to win and supposed the defences they possessed were adequate. It is after this defeat that the temper and mood of the English slides into defeatism and division" (174). The diplomatic victory in the Norman negotiations would therefore seem to be overshadowed by the military disaster at Maldon, but we must bear in mind that there were ongoing negotiations with the Scandinavians, too. Maldon in fact precipitated a treaty, still extant, between Ethelred and the leading viking chieftains Olaf Tryggvason, Justin, and Guthmund. The terms of the treaty were reviewed with a rancor undiminished by nine centuries in T. D. Kendrick's viking history:

> Æthelred, whose miserable sobriquet was to be 'the Redeless,' the king who was *lacking in counsel,* did not hasten to avenge the death of these loyal men of Essex. Instead it was resolved, on the advice of Sigeric, Archbishop of Canterbury, to make peace with the viking leaders, and by a bribe of 10,000 pounds of silver to obtain from them a promise that they would not molest the southern English again and that they would help to ward off any other viking attacks that occurred while they and their fleet remained in Essex. But this was not the whole of the shameful bargain, for in addition to the very heavy tribute (danegeld) thus

offered, Æthelred further promised to supply rations for the pirate force while the vikings stayed in England. Thus was danger temporarily averted by a cowardly and ill-omened pact. It was not, of course, the first occasion whereupon English money had been paid to the Northmen, but it was the first bribe of the sort that openly revealed the English king as a weakling and his English subjects as no longer a hardy and implacable foe [260].

What Kendrick wrote under the influence of an age-old grievance against King Ethelred was in fact a skewed reading of the treaty. We may consider just one sentence in the first paragraph: "And gif ænig sciphere on Englaland hergie, þæt we habban heora ealra fultum; and we him sculon mete findan, þa hwile þe hy mid us beoð" ("And if any naval force harries in England, we shall have the assistance of all of them; and we shall provide food for them for the time they are with us"; see Schmid 204; Liebermann 1.222; Robertson 56). In other words, the provisioning is in return for, and coterminous with, the military aid provided by Olaf and his followers against other vikings, a point that gets lost in Kendrick's rendering. It appears that Ethelred is pursuing exactly the same policy in this treaty that he pursued in his Norman treaty of the same year: he is trying to divide the enemy, win over Olaf Tryggvason and his followers, and turn them against other viking enemies.

It must be admitted that this sensible policy did not succeed in the short run and that Olaf returned in 994 in league with Swein Forkbeard of Denmark to make an abortive assault on London, then to ravage in Essex, Kent, Sussex, and Hampshire. But Ethelred persisted in his policy of three years earlier—some persistence is, after all, what constitutes policy. He again paid tribute, this time in the amount of sixteen thousand pounds, and he provisioned the whole force on English soil during the winter. We are not told by the *Anglo-Saxon Chronicle* that the pact was a defensive one, but the treaty of 991 might lead us to believe it was. Ethelred subsequently dispatched Bishop Ælfheah and Ealdorman Æthelweard to bring Olaf to Andover, where, the *Chronicle* says, "King Ethelred stood sponsor to him at confirmation, and bestowed gifts on him royally. And then Olaf promised—as also he performed— that he would never come back to England in hostility" (Whitelock 235–36). In short, on his second attempt King Ethelred succeeded utterly. He was able to separate Olaf from the viking cause, just as he was able to detach Thorkell the Tall from the Danish invasion twenty years later. His personal success with Olaf is, oddly enough, commemorated more fondly in Scandinavia than in England. In the *Great Saga of Olaf Tryggvason* (chapters 285–86) we learn that Ethelred's son Edward the Confessor was always mindful of his father's friendship with Olaf and was in the habit of telling Olaf's story to his retainers every Easter (Halldórsson 1961, 348–49; Ashdown 152–53).

If we look closely at Ethelred's strategy at Andover, we may break

it down into three interlocking components. The first was to confirm
Olaf's Christian allegiance. The second was to form a family alliance
with Olaf. The third was to neutralize him as a military factor. Each
component has its own history.

Religious rapprochement was a natural concomitant of English efforts
to blunt the viking attacks. In 878 (version C, 879) the *Chronicle* tells
us that King Alfred stood godfather at the baptism of Guthrum in his
attempt to stave off the Danish threat: "And then the enemy gave him
preliminary hostages and great oaths that they would leave his kingdom,
and promised also that their king should receive baptism, and they kept
their promise. Three weeks later King Guthrum with 30 of the men who
were the most important in the army came [to him] at Aller, which is
near Athelney, and the king stood sponsor to him at his baptism there;
and the unbinding of the chrism took place at Wedmore. And he was
twelve days with the king, and he honoured him and his companions
greatly with gifts" (Whitelock 196; cf. Keynes and Lapidge 85). Another
precedent can be located during the reign of Athelstan, who fostered the
Norwegian prince Hákon (later Hákon the Good) at his court. Hákon
thus grew up as a Christian and later became the first Christian king of
Norway. R. I. Page speculates that this was indeed the English plan: "A
Christian Norway, if it could be achieved, might provide less formidable
foes than a pagan one" (116; cf. Birkeli 1960).

In point of fact, such a Christian strategy dates back to the beginning
of the Viking Age. As early as 826 the German emperor Louis the Pious
undertook the conversion of a claimant to the Danish throne, Harald
Klak, surely in the hope of pacifying his northern border (Andersson,
esp. 227). Ethelred thus resorted to a well-established policy, but it did
not always achieve the desired ends: Harald Klak failed to make good
his claim in Denmark, and Hákon appears to have apostatized under
pressure from his heathen countrymen. Ethelred, on the other hand, succeeded. The year after his meeting with Olaf at Andover, the latter
launched a lightning conversion of Norway and her dependencies, a conversion that made extraordinary headway in the five short years of his
reign. We can only guess at the extent of English complicity in this
conversion campaign, but it may have been considerable. To my knowledge it has not been suggested that Ethelred had a hand in the conversion
of Norway, but now that he may be viewed as something more than a
somnolescent accessory to disaster, the time has come to weigh the possibility. Some of the mystery surrounding Olaf's quick success in Norway
is dispelled if we imagine that English support was a significant factor.
At the very least we might surmise that some of the sixteen thousand
pounds paid to Olaf in 994 were earmarked for the Norwegian conversion.

The second object of Ethelred's policy was family alliance. When
he met with Olaf at Andover, Olaf was already baptized, although it is
uncertain whether the ceremony occurred in Germany or England. Ethelred

therefore did not stand godfather, as Louis the Pious had done for Harald Klak and Alfred for Guthrum, but was sponsor at a confirmation ceremony. This, too, implied a family relationship and entailed family obligations. Just as Ethelred's Norman negotiations culminated in his marriage with Emma, the sister of Duke Richard II of Normandy, in 1002, so his negotiations with Olaf resulted in the spiritual relationship of sponsor to confirmand. Ethelred thus designed his family network to encompass both Normandy and, on speculation, Norway. For surely, having bound Olaf to him, he was hopeful of, and instrumental in, Olaf's Norwegian conquest. As events turned out, Ethelred's speculation on Olaf's success in Norway was remarkably sound.

The third and final element in Ethelred's strategy was the nullification of Olaf's military threat. He accordingly extracted a promise from Olaf "that he would never come back to England in hostility" (". . .and him þa Anlaf behet, swa he hit eac gelæste þæt he næfre eft to Angelcynne mid unfriðe cuman nolde," Rositzke 54). This stipulation requires close scrutiny. Up until 994 Olaf Tryggvason had been an adventurer, a mercenary, and, if we accept T. D. Kendrick's word, a "pirate." If he did not intend to persist in that career or to press his attacks in England, what *did* he intend to do? His promise to Ethelred would oblige him to dissociate himself from his Danish allies, whose continuing activity was clearly targeted on England. The Baltic arena was controlled by Danes and Swedes, as Olaf was to discover in his final battle six years later. Nor was he offered a fief in England, although he and his host had been provisioned the previous winter in Southampton. Almost by a process of elimination it must have been understood at Andover that Olaf would have Norway. A clear claim to Norway was the logical alternative to settlement in England, and English support of Olaf's Norwegian enterprise must have been part of the bargain, tacit or otherwise. No small part of this support came in the form of sixteen thousand English pounds. In the year 995, then, Norway was in all probability conquered and converted to a large extent with English money, English provisions, and—most assuredly—abundant English blessings.

The meeting of Olaf and Ethelred at Andover was no chance occasion but a link in a consistent English viking policy, a policy pursued in negotiations with the Normans perhaps since 888 (Stafford p. 29, note 78) and in negotiations with Olaf Tryggvason since 991. Ethelred tried repeatedly to relieve viking pressure by treating with individual vikings and integrating them into his defense establishment; that was the point of Danegeld, as the treaty of 991 clearly indicates. Furthermore, it strains credence to believe that Ethelred's cultivation of Olaf and Olaf's conversion of Norway are unconnected. Olaf would not have made peace with Ethelred without knowing his next move. The two leaders thus made a mutually beneficial pact: Ethelred was to help Olaf win Norway, and Olaf was to convert Norway so as to assure tranquility from that quarter.

Olaf got Norway and Ethelred got peace. The plan was sealed with pledges and assurances. Olaf affirmed his Christianity and became Ethelred's confirmand, that is, a member of Ethelred's family—Florence of Worcester says explicitly that Ethelred "adopted him as his son" (Thorpe 152). Henceforward Olaf was bound to him by more than diplomatic ties. Ethelred's pledge was money, sixteen thousand pounds of it, enough to make the conquest of Norway and the work of conversion realistic. It was not just good money thrown after bad, but foreign aid allocated by Ethelred in the interest of securing a friendly neighboring realm.

The lines of Ethelred's foreign policy emerge rather clearly. He sought to guard his flanks, Normandy to the south and Norway to the northeast. That he finally could not resist the waves of head-on assaults from Denmark under Thorkell the Tall, Swein Forkbeard, and King Cnut may say less about his administrative competence than about his misfortune in reigning at a time of extraordinary Danish ascendancy. When Ethelred died on April 13, 1016, the *Chronicle* states simply that "he had held his kingdom with great toil and difficulties as long as his life lasted" (Whitelock 249). That was no mean achievement.

WORKS CITED

Andersson, Theodore M. "The Viking Image in Carolingian Poetry." *Les Relations littéraires franco-scandinaves au moyen âge: Actes du colloque de Liège (avril 1972).* Bibliothèque de la Faculté de Philosophie et Lettres de l'Université de Liège 208. Paris: Belles Lettres, 1975. 217–46.

Ashdown, Margaret. *English and Norse Documents Relating to the Reign of Ethelred the Unready.* 1930. New York: Russell & Russell, 1972.

Birkeli, Fridtjov. "Hadde Håkon Adalsteinsfostre likevel en biskop Sigfrid hos seg?" *(Norsk) Historisk tidskrift* 40 (1960): 113–36.

———, Fridjov [sic]. "The Earliest Missionary Activities from England to Norway." *Nottingham Mediaeval Studies* 15 (1971): 27–37.

Brooks, N. P. "Arms, Status and Warfare in Late-Saxon England." In Hill 81–103.

Dolley, Michael. "An Introduction to the Coinage of Æthelraed II." In Hill 115–33.

Ellehøj, Svend. *Studier over den ældste norrøne historieskrivning.* Bibliotheca Arnamagnæana 26. Copenhagen: Munksgaard, 1965.

Fauroux, Marie, ed. *Recueil des actes des ducs de Normandie (911–1066).* Caen: Société des Antiquaires de Normandie, 1961.

Gem, Richard. "Church Architecture in the Reign of King Æthelred." In Hill 105–14.

Halldórsson, Ólafur. "Óláfs saga Tryggvasonar." *Kulturhistorisk leksikon for nordisk middelalder.* Copenhagen: Rosenkilde and Bagger, 1967. 12:551–53.

———, ed. Vol. 2 of *Óláfs saga Tryggvasonar en mesta.* Editiones Arnamagnæanæ Series A. Copenhagen: Munksgaard, 1961.

Hill, David, ed. *Ethelred the Unready: Papers from the Millenary Conference.* British Archaeological Reports, British Series 59. Oxford: B.A.R., 1978.

John, Eric. "War and Society in the Tenth Century: The Maldon Campaign." *Transactions of the Royal Historical Society* 27 (1977): 173–95.

Kendrick, T. D. [Thomas Downing]. *A History of the Vikings.* 1930. London: Cass, 1968.

Keynes, S. D. [Simon]. "The Declining Reputation of King Æthelred the Unready." In Hill 227–53.

_____. *The Diplomas of King Æthelred 'The Unready' 978–1016: A Study in Their Use as Historical Evidence*. Cambridge Studies in Medieval Life and Thought, Third Series 13. Cambridge: Cambridge University Press, 1980.

Keynes, Simon, and Michael Lapidge, trans. *Alfred the Great: Asser's Life of King Alfred and Other Contemporary Sources*. Harmondsworth: Penguin, 1983.

Kipling, Rudyard. *Rudyard Kipling's Verse: Definitive Edition*. Garden City, N.Y.: Doubleday, 1940.

Liebermann, F. [Felix], ed. Vol. I of *Die Gesetze der Angelsachsen*. Halle: Niemeyer, 1898.

Logue, Christopher, and Bert Kitchen. *Abecedary*. London: Jonathan Cape, n.d.

Lönnroth, Lars. "Studier i Olaf Tryggvasons saga." *Samlaren* 84 (1963): 54–94.

Maurer, Konrad. Vol. I of *Die Bekehrung des norwegischen Stammes zum Christenthume*. 1855. Osnabrück: Otto Zeller, 1965.

Metcalf, D. M. "The Ranking of the Boroughs: Numismatic Evidence from the Reign of Æthelred II." In Hill 159–212.

Page, R. I. "The Audience of *Beowulf* and the Vikings." *The Dating of Beowulf*. Ed. Colin Chase. Toronto: University of Toronto Press, 1981. 113–22.

Robertson, A. J. [Agnes Jane], ed. and trans. *The Laws of the Kings of England from Edmund to Henry I*. Cambridge: Cambridge University Press, 1925.

Rositzke, Harry August, ed. *The C-Text of the Old English Chronicles*. Beiträge zur englischen Philologie 34. Bochum-Langendreer: Heinrich Pöppinghaus, 1940.

Schmid, Reinhold, ed. *Die Gesetze der Angelsachsen*. Leipzig: Brockhaus, 1858.

Stafford, Pauline. "The Reign of Æthelred II, a Study in the Limitations on Royal Policy and Action." In Hill 15–46.

Thorpe, Benjamin, ed. Vol. I of *Florentii Wigorniensis Monachi Chronicon ex Chronicis*. London: English Historical Society, 1848.

Whitelock, Dorothy, ed. *English Historical Documents, Vol. I (c. 550–1042)*. 2nd ed. London: Eyre and Methuen, 1979.

Wormald, Patrick. "Æthelred the Lawmaker." In Hill 47–80.

THE VIKING POLICY OF ETHELRED: A RESPONSE

PHYLLIS R. BROWN
Santa Clara University

P ROFESSOR ANDERSSON'S PAPER is an excellent corrective: we tend simply to accept tradition and dismiss Ethelred as "unready" despite the certain inappropriateness of that epithet. His essay demonstrates that, especially in the 990s, Ethelred attempted to establish a policy to deal with the Scandinavian threat. However, from our historical perspective, Ethelred does seem to have been ill advised. Several events from the later years of Ethelred's reign reveal some basic weaknesses in his policy.

On St. Brice's day (November 13) in the year 1002, according to his own admission, Ethelred ordered that all Danes in England be killed (Whitelock 238–39, 591). There could have been no realistic expectation that such an order would or could be carried out absolutely, especially in places like Dane-occupied York. It is at least questionable policy to order actions that are beyond one's power to execute. A more specific problem in this instance, however, resulted from the identity of one of the victims of that order: Gunnhild, sister of Swein Forkbeard. Stenton speculates that Swein's desire for vengeance for the murder of his sister was an important motive behind his harrying of England in 1004 (380). Although Ethelred could scarcely have foreseen all the implications of his attempted massacre, that result strikes one as particularly predictable. Here we have an example, if not of an ill-advised action, at least of one inconsistent with his policy of buying off the vikings and assisting them— and Olaf, in particular— with other enterprises in order to deflect their aggressive activities from England.

Second, in 1007 Ethelred revived the Mercian ealdormanry, probably in an attempt to improve the defense of Mercia and thus of all of central England. While the policy may have been excellent, his choice of Eadric as ealdorman was less successful. Subsequently Eadric was more helpful to the Danish invaders than to Ethelred. As the *Anglo-Saxon Chronicle* recounts for the year 1009,

> Then on one occasion the king had intercepted them [the Danes] with all his army, when they wished to go to their ships, and the whole people was ready to attack them, but it was hindered by

Ealdorman Eadric, then as it always was [Whitelock 242].

There is some evidence that Eadric's reputation before his appointment was not impeccable. Florence of Worcester's *Chronicle* hints that Eadric was responsible for the murder of a Northumbrian ealdorman, Elfhelm (Stenton 382). If this evidence is reliable, Ethelred's policy was undercut by a bad appointment, certainly an important element in policy.

The years 1008–09 offer another instructive incident. In 1008 Ethelred ordered that a new fleet of warships be built. Again this seems excellent policy, but again an administrative appointment subverted it. The next year Wulfnoth, one of the commanders, took twenty ships of the new fleet and began harrying the south coast of England. Another commander, Brihtric (Eadric's brother), took eighty ships in an attempt to capture Wulfnoth and thereby "make a big reputation for himself" (in the words of the C version of the *Chronicle*); a storm hit and blew all his ships onto shore; then Wulfnoth burned whatever was left of them (Whitelock 242).

These examples suggest that whenever Ethelred had a policy that we can applaud from our perspective, something went wrong with it, usually as a result of some inconsistency with regard to it, as with the massacre of St. Brice's Day and the unwise appointments of Eadric and Wulfnoth. Even Thorkell the Tall's service to Ethelred in 1012, which Andersson cites as another example of Ethelred's policy of dividing the vikings in an attempt to weaken their force, can be seen as having mixed results, for Swein's attack in 1013, according to Stenton, was principally motivated by a desire to "punish Thorkell for his defection" (Stenton 384). Furthermore, Thorkell's abandonment of the Danish attacks on England may have been a result more of his disgust at the Danish murder of Archbishop Elfheah, as Stenton suggests (383–84), than of any particular policy on Ethelred's part.

This evidence leads me to suggest that although Ethelred may well have been attempting to establish a policy for the viking problem in the 990s, his actions and policies in the following thirteen years suggest that he was indeed *unræd*—if not "lacking in counsel," at least "ill advised." Even his assistance to Olaf, which according to Andersson could have been instrumental in Olaf's successes between 995 and 1000, seems to have worked out better for the Scandinavians than for the English.

The entry in the C version of the *Anglo-Saxon Chronicle* for the year 1011 calls emphatic attention to the weakness of Ethelred's foreign policy during at least the last thirteen years of his reign:

> In this year the king and his councillors sent to the army and asked for peace, and promised them tribute and provisions on condition that they should cease their ravaging. They had then overrun: (i) East Anglia, (ii) Essex, (iii) Middlesex, (iv) Oxford-shire, (v) Cambridgeshire, (vi) Hertfordshire, (vii) Buckingham-

shire, (viii) Bedfordshire, (ix) half Huntingdonshire, (x) much of Northamptonshire; and south of the Thames all Kent, Sussex, Hastings, Surrey, Berkshire, Hampshire and much of Wiltshire. All those disasters befell us through bad policy, in that they were never offered tribute in time nor fought against; but when they had done most to our injury, peace and truce were made with them; and for all this truce and tribute they journeyed none the less in bands everywhere, and harried our wretched people, and plundered and killed them [Whitelock 244].

The inconsistency or inadequacy of Ethelred's policy brought worse and worse disaster to the English as his reign progressed. What was good for Olaf was not necessarily good for the English.

WORKS CITED

Stenton, Frank M. *Anglo-Saxon England.* 3rd ed. Oxford: Clarendon, 1971.
Whitelock, Dorothy, ed. *English Historical Documents: Volume I c. 500–1042.* 2nd ed. London: Eyre and Methuen, 1979.

ETHELRED II, OLAF TRYGGVASON, AND THE CONVERSION OF NORWAY

PETER SAWYER
Alingsås, Sweden

T HE MILLENIUM of Ethelred's accession was marked by the publication of a most valuable collection of papers in which belated justice was done to that much maligned and misunderstood monarch. It is a matter of regret that that book is already out of print, and we may be grateful to Theodore Andersson for having reported many of the main points made in those essays in his contribution to the present volume. Fortunately Simon Keynes's very thorough and readable study *The Diplomas of King Æthelred "The Unready," 978–1016*, which has a much wider interest than its title may suggest, is still available. It should be required reading not only for historians of Anglo-Saxon England but also for students of Old English literature, so much of which derives from Ethelred's reign.

Andersson's contribution to the rehabilitation of Ethelred concerns the king's foreign policy, which, he suggests, was "designed to neutralize the Norwegian vikings by converting them to religious like-mindedness and calculated to drive a wedge between Norwegians and Danes, thus dividing the attackers." The crucial event in the implementation of this policy was Olaf's confirmation, with Ethelred as sponsor. After this, in the words of the *Anglo-Saxon Chronicle*, Ethelred "bestowed gifts on him royally. And Olaf promised—as he also performed—that he would never come back to England in hostility." Andersson suggests that "the two leaders thus made a mutually beneficial pact: Ethelred was to help Olaf win Norway, and Olaf was to convert Norway so as to assure tranquility from that quarter."

The pacifying effects of Christianity may be doubted. The conversion of the Danes, for example, does not seem to have reduced their eagerness to pillage the English. There is less doubt about the effect of Olaf's success in Norway on his relations with Swein; a few years later Olaf was defeated and killed in battle against his former companion. On the other hand, there is nothing to suggest that the alliance between Olaf and Swein was more than a temporary agreement to join forces for the attack on London in 994. The only viking leader mentioned later in the annal for that year is Olaf, and it seems likely that he and Swein parted company after their failure to take London, or at least before Olaf's army took up winter quarters in Southampton. The *Chronicle* does not mention Swein again until his return in 1003.

If the treaty between Ethelred and a viking army led by Olaf, Jostein, and Guthmund was concluded after the campaigns of 994, as seems likely (Liebermann 1: 220–25, trans. Whitelock 437–39), the probability is strengthened that Swein, who is not mentioned in the treaty, was no longer with the army and had probably left England. It has been argued by Liebermann and, following him, by many others that this treaty belongs to 991 and follows the so-called Maldon campaign (149–50). One of Liebermann's arguments was that Swein is not mentioned in the treaty, but a more important reason is that Archbishop Sigeric, who is named as one of those who negotiated the treaty, died on 28 October 994. But as E. V. Gordon pointed out in 1937, the text of the treaty shows that Sigeric was one of the leaders who concluded local truces with the vikings before the general peace was agreed. The first clause reads,

> Firstly, that a general peace be established between King Ethelred with all his people and all the army to which the king gave the tribute, according to the terms which Archbishop Sigeric, Ealdorman Æthelweard (of the Western Provinces of Wessex) and Ealdorman Ælfric (of Hampshire) made, when they obtained permission from the king to purchase peace for the areas which they had rule over, under the king [Whitelock 437].

As Gordon remarked, "the statement that local truces had been purchased by Sigeric, Æthelweard and Ælfric is strong evidence that the treaty belongs to 994 and not to 991, since the districts governed by them were all ravaged in 994, but only that of Sigeric (and Byrhtnoth) in 991" (27–28). Gordon also countered Liebermann's other arguments and drew the reasonable conclusion that the treaty belongs to 994. The figure it gives for the tribute paid to the viking army, 22,000 pounds, does not agree with the payments stated in the *Chronicle* for either 991 or 994, which are 10,000 and 16,000 pounds, respectively. The probable explanation for the discrepancy is that the treaty includes the sums paid locally before the general peace was bought. There is independent charter evidence for a payment of tribute to vikings by Archbishop Sigeric in 994 (Whitelock 571–73).

There is also charter evidence to suggest that Swein was in England sometime before 994. An undated charter of Ethelred, which must have been drawn up between 995 and 999, confirms the will of Æthelric of Bocking, in Essex, who was suspected of complicity in a conspiracy to receive Swein "in Essex when first he came there with a fleet" (Whitelock 580); the wording of this text makes it very unlikely that the campaign of 994 was meant:

It was many years before Æthelric died that the king was told
that he was concerned in the treacherous plan that Sven should
be received in Essex when first he came there with a fleet; and
the king before many witnesses informed Archbishop Sigeric of
it, who was then his advocate for the sake of the estate at Bocking
which he had bequeathed to Christ Church. Then, both during his
life and afterwards, he was neither cleared of this charge, nor was
the crime atoned for.

There is, however, no reason to assume that Swein's first visit was in
991, in the company of Olaf. It could have been at any time. The
Chronicle for that period was compiled after Ethelred's death (Keynes
1978, 229–32), and there are several indications that its record of raids
in the early part of the reign is incomplete. It seems unlikely, for example,
that Ethelred would have begun negotiations with the Duke of Normandy
as early as 988 to prevent his enemies finding shelter in the Duchy if
the only raids were those reported in the *Chronicle*, namely, for the years
980, 981, 982, and 988 (Keynes 1980, 91, note 29; Whitelock 894–95).

The evidence for Swein's early years is unsatisfactory and contradic-
tory (Skovgaard-Petersen). There was a widespread tradition that sometime after the death of his father, Harold, he was driven into exile, but
the details are lost in legend (Campbell, li, note 9). It is possible that
he was an exile when he first came to England, but by the end of the
century he had certainly established himself as his father's heir, and he
led the coalition against Olaf Tryggvason.

The early career of Olaf Tryggvason is no less obscure, despite the
full accounts preserved in Norwegian and Icelandic texts. They all agree
that he was of distant royal descent and that he was taken into exile as
a baby by his mother, for safety. After many adventures he emerges as
the leader of a viking fleet raiding in the Baltic, the British Isles, and
elsewhere. The main evidence for these campaigns appears to be the
poem *Óláfsdrápa* by Hallfrøðr Vandræðaskáld (Jónsson 156–59, pt. A;
148–50, pt. B), but we cannot hope for an impartial account in praise
poetry of this kind. There is the further difficulty that several episodes
in the Icelandic sagas about Olaf Tryggvason appear to have been transferred to him from earlier lives of St. Olaf Haraldsson, a transposition
that has been convincingly demonstrated by Lars Lönnroth. One episode,
concerning Olaf's baptism, is particularly relevant here. The earliest version is in the late twelfth-century Norwegian text *Ágrip*:

But the end of all these exploits was that he [Olaf Tryggvason]
landed in England, at a certain place where lived a great friend
of God, a hermit, famed for his excellent learning and various
knowledge. Olaf was eager to test this, and dressed one of his
retainers like a king, so that under the name of a king he might
seek [the hermit's] advice. Now this was the answer he received:

"You are no king, and my counsel to you is that you should be
loyal to your king." When Olaf heard this answer, he was yet
more eager to see him, because he no longer doubted that he was
a true prophet. . .[Ashdown 146–47].

The hermit then told Olaf, "You will be a famous king, and do famous
deeds. You will bring many peoples to faith and baptism, thereby profiting
yourself and many others." He further prophesied that Olaf would be
ambushed and wounded but would recover in seven days, "and soon after
you will receive baptism" (149). This incident was later elaborated by
Snorri Sturlusson, who placed the encounter with the hermit and the
baptism in the Scilly Isles (Aðalbjarnarson 266–67). The first part of this
story is based on one told about St. Benedict and the Gothic king Totila
by Gregory the Great in book 2, chapter 14 of his *Dialogues* (Gardner
73–74; Lönnroth 60–61). According to Gregory, Totila later went to
Sicily, and this probably explains Snorri's reference to the Scilly Isles.
The more important point is that this story had earlier been told about
St. Olaf.

One may suspect a similar transfer underlying the story, related in
the longer saga of Olaf Tryggvason, that Edward the Confessor made it
his custom on the first day of Easter to retell to his chief men and courtiers
the saga of Olaf Tryggvason. "He said that he related the tale of King
Olaf on Easter day rather than on any other day, because, as he declared,
Olaf Tryggvason surpassed other kings as Easter Day is better than other
days in the twelve months" (Ashdown 152–53). The reason for these
transfers is partly, as Lönnroth suggests, that the people of Tröndelag
deliberately built up Olaf Tryggvason as a hero to counter St. Olaf, who
had died at their hands. Another powerful factor tending to produce the
same result was the Icelandic belief, first expressed by Ari Þorgilsson in
the early twelfth century, that the Icelanders officially accepted Christianity in the year 1000 (Benediktsson ch. 7, headings 14–18). The millenium
is perhaps a suspicious date, but there is little doubt that Christianity was
received at about that time, within the lifetime of Ari's informants. Some
Icelanders would probably have been happier to associate the event with
St. Olaf rather than Olaf Tryggvason, but that was chronologically impossible. What is more, the method of persuasion supposed to have been
used by the Norwegian king—a threat to maim and kill all Icelanders in
Norway—would not have fitted well with the heroic image of the saint.
Such brutal evangelism was more easily attributed to Olaf Tryggvason,
who is generally presented in a less than favorable light in the Icelandic
sagas devoted to him.

Ari's date for the acceptance of Christianity in Iceland may be roughly
correct, but many details of his story are dubious. It is unlikely, for
example, that Olaf Tryggvason's power in Norway was sufficiently extensive to make his threat to Icelanders very effective. Another curious
element in Ari's story is the analogy used by the Lawspeaker Thorgeirr:

He related how the kings of Norway and Denmark had carried
on war and battles between them for a long time, till the people
of those countries made peace between them, even though they
themselves did not want it. And that policy answered so well that
in no time at all they were sending each other precious gifts, and
peace was maintained for the rest of their lives [Jones 107–08].

One wonders which kings and what period Thorgeirr had in mind. The
argument seems particularly inappropriate at the very time that the Danish
Swein was destroying Olaf. Perhaps Ari was influenced by the relatively
peaceful relations between Norway and Denmark in his own time.

An alternative date for the conversion of Iceland is given by Adam
of Bremen in book 4 of his *Gesta Hammaburgensis*, chapter 36 (Trillmich
486, cf. 424). He claims that it was the work of Adalbert, who was
archbishop of Hamburg-Bremen from 1043 to 1072. This dating is consistent with Adam's attitude throughout his work; proper order, in his
eyes, required submission to the archbishop of Hamburg-Bremen. Whatever Christian missionaries had been active in Iceland earlier, it was
Ísleifr's consecration by Adalbert that established regular ecclesiastical
order there. When Ari was writing, the metropolitan authority of Hamburg-
Bremen had been challenged by the creation of the archbishropic of Lund,
and it may be significant that Ari does not say where or by whom any
Icelandic bishops were consecrated. He certainly does not acknowledge
any claim by Hamburg-Bremen.

The emphasis put on the Norwegian initiative may have been in part
a reaction to the claims of the German and, perhaps, the Danish archbish-
ropics, but it must also have been affected by the Icelandic interest in
Norwegian kings. Despite the belief cherished by some Icelanders that
their ancestors had emigrated to escape royal tyranny, other Icelanders
served Norwegian kings as warriors or sang their praise as poets. Church-
men, too, were eager to emphasize the royal basis of their church, and
Ari himself wrote about the lives of Norwegian kings, a text that has
unfortunately not survived (Benediktsson 3). That combination of factors
made it desirable, even necessary, to cast Olaf Tryggvason in the role
of a missionary king, and in the process stories first told about St. Olaf
were transferred to his namesake.

Olaf Tryggvason's supposed role in the conversion of Iceland was,
of course, an extension of his evangelism in Norway. But there are several
indications that at least the coastal region of Norway had already been
greatly affected by Christianity long before his time. The well-attested
relations between Harold Fairhair and Athelstan, which included Harold's
sending his son Hákon to be brought up in the court of that most Christian
king (Stenton 344–45; Whitelock 303–10), suggests that Norway was
already open to Christian influence in the early part of the tenth century.
The abandonment of traditional burial customs at that time by the coastal

communities of Norway was not necessarily due to Christian influence, but that seems the most likely explanation (Rolfsen). The inclusion of *Sigefridus Norwegensis episcopus* among the obits of Glastonbury monks who were bishops in the time of King Edgar, who died in 975, is good evidence for the presence of an English mission in Norway in the tenth century (Scott 138).[1] The complex of later traditions about English missionaries called Sigfrid in eleventh-century Scandinavia probably derived some of their force from the memory of this early missionary bishop (Schmid).

According to the saga about him, Hákon, "Athelstan's fosterling," was a Christian who was forced to compromise his religion (Aðalbjarnarson, esp. 171–73, 192–97). While this account may be true, it is equally likely to be a construction made necessary by the role assigned to Olaf Tryggvason. Little weight should be put on the tradition that the opposition to Hákon was a pagan reaction. Such interpretations are a familiar *topos* in histories of conversion; see, for example, the opposition to Olaf Skötkonung (Trillmich 296–98) and to King Ingi (Tolkien 62–63), and the examples from Islamic history (see Levtzion 6).

Adam of Bremen's comments on Olaf Tryggvason in book 2, chapter 40, are equally suspect. According to Adam,

> Some relate that Olaf had been a Christian, some that he had forsaken Christianity; all, however, affirm that he was skilled in divination, was an observer of the lots, and had placed all his hopes in the prognostication of birds. Wherefore, also, did he receive a byname, so that he was called Craccaben. In fact, as they say, he also was given to the practice of the magic art and supported as his household companions all the magicians with whom that land was overrun and, deceived by their error, perished
> [Trillmich 276, trans. Tschan 82].

Adam's attitude may have been influenced by his informant, the Danish king Sven Estrithsen, but a more powerful reason for his denigration of Olaf was the Norwegian refusal to accept the authority of Hamburg-Bremen. Adam's "magicians" may indeed have been missionaries who paid no heed to the claims of Adam's church.

We have no reason to doubt that Olaf Tryggvason was converted, baptized (probably in Norway, see Trillmich 272–74), and episcopally confirmed at Andover in the spring of 995. With his newly won wealth and reputation he conquered Tröndelag. In *Ólafsdrápa*, a poem composed to mourn his death, he is called lord of the people of Tröndelag.[2] He was a Norwegian king, not king of Norway, and his significance as unifier of, and evangelist in, Norway can easily be exaggerated. Ethelred was doubtless delighted to see the back of him, but his removal from the English scene did not make much difference. There were many other Scandinavian bands eager to exploit England's weakness, a weakness that owed more to the stresses and tensions of a recently unified kingdom than to the incompetence of the English king. The confirmation of Olaf was a notable event, and was duly noted, but Ethelred had other and more significant allies, including St. Olaf himself, who helped him recover power after the death of Swein Forkbeard in 1014 (Campbell 78–82). This latter Olaf also went on to Norway, where in his turn he had to face opposition powerfully supported by Swein's son Cnut, who could draw on the wealth of England as its king.

Ethelred's relations with the Olafs should be seen against the background of friendly contacts between England and Norway that went back at least to the time of Athelstan and were greatly strengthened by the activities of English missionaries like Sigfrid. We cannot know what Ethelred and his advisers hoped for from their dealings with those Norwegian leaders, but their "foreign policy" towards both Normandy and Norway certainly had some useful immediate results. It was, however, in the long term that those dealings proved momentous, on the battlefields of Stamford Bridge and Hastings in 1066.

¹ Cf. Birkeli. The rubric referring to Edgar applies only to the first part of the list, in which Sigfrid appears as the fourth, between Ælfweald and Æthelwold, who died in 972 and 984, respectively.

² The poem is printed in Jónsson 159–66, pt A; 150–57, pt B; with an English translation in Ashdown 126–35. The relevant verse is no. 23. The reading *þrœnda* is, however, doubtful. It is an emendation of the manuscript reading *þegn*(ar).

WORKS CITED

Andersson, Theodore M. "The Viking Policy of Ethelred the Unready." *Scandinavian Studies* 58.3 (1987): in the present volume.

Ashdown, Margaret. *English and Norse Documents Relating to the Reign of Ethelred the Unready.* 1930. New York: Russell & Russell, 1972.

Aðalbjarnarson, Bjarni, ed. Snorri Sturluson, "Heimskringla." Íslensk fornrit 36. 2 vols. Reykjavik: Hið Íslenzka fornritafélag, 1941–51.

Benediktsson, Jakob, ed. *Íslendingabók, Landnámabók.* Íslensk fornrit 1. Reykjavik: Hið Íslenzka fornritafélag, 1968.

Birkeli, Fridjov. "The Earliest Missionary Activity from England to Norway." *Nottingham Mediaeval Studies* 15 (1971): 27–37.

Campbell, Alistair, ed. *Encomium Emmae Reginae.* London: Royal Historical Society, 1949.

Gardner, Edmund G., ed. *The Dialogues of St. Gregory the Great.* London: Wormer, 1911.

Gordon, E. V. "The Date of Æthelred's Treaty with the Vikings: Olaf Tryggvason and the Battle of Maldon." *Modern Language Review* 32 (1937): 24–32.

Jones, Gwyn. *The Norse Atlantic Saga.* London: Oxford, 1964.

Jónsson, Finnur, ed. *Den Norske-Islandske Skjaldedigtning.* Copenhagen: Nordisk forlag, 1912–15.

Hill, David, ed. *Ethelred the Unready: Papers from the Millenary Conference.* British Archaeological Reports, British Series 59. Oxford: B.A.R., 1978.

Keynes, Simon. "The Declining Reputation of King Æthelred the Unready." In Hill 227–53.

_____. *The Diplomas of King Æthelred 'The Unready' 978–1016: A Study in Their Use as Historical Evidence.* Cambridge Studies in Medieval Life and Thought, Third Series 13. Cambridge: Cambridge University Press, 1980.

Levtzion, Nehemia, ed. *Conversion to Islam.* New York: Holmes and Meier, 1979.

Liebermann, F. [Felix], ed. *Die Gesetze der Angelsachsen.* 3 vols. Halle: Niemeyer, 1903–16.

Lönnroth, Lars. "Studier i Olaf Tryggvasons saga." *Samlaren* 84 (1963): 56–94.

Rolfsen, P. "Den siste hedning på Agder." *Viking* 44 (1981): 112–28.

Schmid, Toni. *Den helige Sigfrid.* Lund: Gleerup, 1931.

Scott, John. *The Early History of Glastonbury: An Edition, Translation and Study of William of Malmesbury's "De antiquitate Glastonis ecclesie."* Woodbridge: Boydell Press, 1981.

Sisam, Kenneth. *Studies in the History of Old English Literature.* Oxford: Clarendon, 1953.

Skovgaard-Petersen, Inge. "Sven Tveskæg i den ældste danske historiografi. En Saxostudie." *Middelalderstudier. Tilegnede Aksel E. Christensen på tresårsdagen 11. september 1966.* Copenhagen: Munksgaard, 1966. 1–38.

Stenton, F. M. *Anglo-Saxon England.* 2nd ed. Oxford: Clarendon, 1947.

Tolkien, Christopher, ed. and trans. *The Saga of King Heidrek the Wise.* London: Nelson, 1960.

Trillmich, Werner, and Rudolph Buchner, eds. "Adam Bremensis: Gesta Hammaburgensis ecclesiae pontificum." In their *Quellen des 9. und 11. Jahrhunderts zur Geschichte der Hamburgischen Kirche und des Reiches.* Berlin: Rütten and Loerning, 1981. 137–499.

Tschan, F. J. *History of the Archbishops of Hamburg-Bremen by Adam of Bremen.* New York: Columbia University Press, 1959.

Whitelock, Dorothy, ed. *English Historical Documents: Volume I, c. 550–1042.* 2nd ed. London: Eyre and Methuen, 1979.

NORSE MYTHOLOGY AND NORTHUMBRIA:
METHODOLOGICAL NOTES

JOHN LINDOW

University of California, Berkeley

SCHOLARS HAVE EXPENDED much energy over the question of the origin or ultimate "home" of Norse mythology or its specific aspects or texts. Long ago Sophus Bugge argued, reasonably skillfully in my opinion, that much of Norse mythology and, indeed, much of Norse literary culture derived from Celtic and Germanic Britain, with England as the link. More recently, others have added to the evidence. This essay considers the efforts of two of them, Hans Kuhn and Wolfgang Butt.[1]

Kuhn's arguments go back at least to his essay on North Germanic paganism in the early Christian era (1942), a paganism to which he assigned a large amount of syncretism. A likely breeding ground for such syncretism was tenth-century England, specifically the Danelaw, and in subsequent articles Kuhn argued the existence of various aspects of that syncretism, advancing the argument perhaps farthest in his article "Rund um die *Vǫluspá*."

As it may be extrapolated from these articles and others, the argument may be divided into four main parts.

1. The kenning type *sverð-Freyr* 'sword-Freyr' or 'man' shows a new and less awed attitude toward the gods. The first attestation of the kenning type is in Egill Skallagrímsson's *Hǫfuðlausn*, which according to tradition was composed in York during the mid-tenth century.

2. The terms *alfaðir* 'all-father' and *sigfaðir* 'victory-father' are applied to Odin (Óðinn). They differ fundamentally from the compounds in *-fǫðr* (which Kuhn derives from IE *potis*, Gothic *faþs* 'lord') and suggest influence of the Christian God. *Sigfaðir* is attested in *Vǫluspá* 55 and *Lokasenna* 58 (where, however, it is used mockingly). *Alfaðir* is attested in *Helgakviða Hundingsbana I* 38—a poem with demonstrable connections with England—and in the work of two eleventh-century Icelandic skalds.

3. Kennings of the type *farma gautr* 'god of loads, of freight' for Odin suggest the reinvigoration of the old pagan myth of Odin's self-sacrifice in light of the crucifixion. The *gautr* complex must be understood

as associated with a more general reinterpretation of Odin in light of the Christian god.

4. A new conception of Valhǫll as Odin's splendid hall emerges along with the new Odin and replaces the grim conception of Valhǫll as the corpses on the battlefield. The first attestation of *Valhǫll*, with this or any other conception, and of simplex *hǫll*, which Kuhn regards as an English loan, is in *Eiríksmál*, a tenth-century poem also associated with Northumbria; Kuhn accepts the poem as composed there.

The evidence associating Kuhn's perceived innovations in Norse mythology with mid-tenth-century England is then primarily textual—or, more accurately, textual/contextual. The first attestations of relevant phenomena appear to be assignable to Northumbria around the middle of the tenth century.

By 1971, writing on Helmut de Boor's seminal contribution to our understanding of the religious language of *Vǫluspá* and of the language of the skalds of the Hlaðir jarls during the mid-tenth century, Kuhn was ready to acknowledge the possibility of innovations within religious language and sought to connect them as well as central cosmological myths to the Northumbrian milieu.

> Es liegt deshalb nah zu vermuten, dass auch die Neuerungen in der religiösen Sprache auf die de Boor vor 40 Jahren unsere Aufmerksamkeit gelenkt hat, mitsamt dem, was unter ihren steht, dort drüben ihre erste Entwicklung erfahren haben. . .[7].

> (It therefore seems natural to presume that, in addition, the innovations in religious language to which de Boor drew our attention forty years ago, together with what stands behind them, experienced their first development there [in England]. . . .)

> Die Eiríkrsmál sind das erste zeitlich und raumlich fixierbar Gedicht, das den Walhallglauben bezeugt, daneben aber auch die Vorstellung vom drohenden Weltuntergang und den mythus von Balders Tod. Sie gehören alle zu den zentralen Themen der Vǫluspá und ihrer eddischen Trabanten, so daß wir vom stofflichen her die Eiríksmál wohl als das früheste datierbare Denkmal dieses Kreises zählen dürfen [11].

> (*Eiríksmál* is the first datable and localizable poem that attests not only belief in Valhǫll, but also the conception of the impending end of the world and the myth of Baldr's death. They all pertain to the central themes of *Vǫluspá* and related eddic poems, and thus from its content we may indeed consider *Eiríksmál* the oldest datable work of this circle.)

Enormous claims are being made here. How solid is the textual/contextual evidence on which they are based?

We may begin by dismissing the validity of *Hǫfuðlausn* as the first attestation of kennings of the *sverð-Freyr* type. Even without the philological evidence that may put the poem in the twelfth century (see, for example, Helgason 1969), the existence of many other head-ransom poems in Old Norse alone makes it clear that we are dealing with a traditional motif whose value as a source is highly suspect. It is far more likely that the most famous of the older skalds, Egill Skallagrímsson, should have had such a story attached to him than that he should have been a model for stories applied to lesser known skalds.

Without *Hǫfuðlausn*, kennings of the *sverð-Freyr* type become the property of the skalds of the Hlaðir jarls, and it is precisely the relationship of the language of these skalds to English tradition that Kuhn seeks to demonstrate. If the argument is to succeed, therefore, it must turn on *Eiríksmál*, and it is indeed on that poem that Kuhn based the most far-ranging statement of his thesis.

Was *Eiríksmál* then composed in Northumbria? And what is its English connection?

Eric Bloodaxe did, indeed, reign in York on two short occasions and was deposed in 954; this we have from the *Anglo-Saxon Chronicle*. He was slain in the same year at Stainmore. At least off and on, he may have been in Northumbria or elsewhere in England between his departure from Norway during the 930s, after the death of Harold Fairhair, and his assumption of the kingdom of York in 948. Furthermore, his father had sent Eric's half-brother, Hákon, to be fostered by Athelstan of England.

Eric seems to have been something of an anomaly in the largely Hiberno-Norse York and was apparently unpopular, since the Northumbrians themselves expelled him. It is therefore perhaps unlikely that the opportunities for cultural and religious influence were very extensive.

As for the composition of the poem, *Fagrskinna* reports that Eric's widow, Gunnhildr, ordered it composed after his death. In the first place, it is possible that the account in *Fagrskinna* is false. The poem is openly pagan, and since the Christian authors of the Icelandic sources are uniformly critical of Gunnhildr, they might have concocted the story so as to associate her with a pagan document and thus vilify her. On the other hand, if there is any truth to the portrait these sources paint of Gunnhildr, she may well have requested not just a praise poem, but a highly pagan one. Indeed, her nominally Christian husband had been slain by forces with a highly Christian orientation.

In any case, if we accept the account in *Fagrskinna*, the poem was commissioned by a Dane for a Norwegian. Although the poet's identity is unknown, he evidently was familiar with eddic and skaldic tradition, and the handbooks take him to be Norwegian (Lie 1953). The account in *Fagrskinna* leaves some doubt as to whether the poem was actually composed in England. In introducing the poem, it states that Gunnhildr commissioned it "eptir fall Eiríks" ("after Eric's death")—how soon after, we do not know. After quoting the poem, however, the author continues:

After King Eric's death, King Edmund was hostile toward Gunnhildr and the sons of Eric. He brought forward as the reason for
it that Eric had harried the interior of the king's [Edmund's] realm.
Gunnhildr then left England for Denmark with her sons. . .

[Trans. of Munch and Unger 18].

The collocation of "eptir fall Eiríks" with the commissioning of the poem
and Gunnhildr's flight to Denmark leaves open the possibility that *Eiríksmál* was composed in Denmark.

There are two additional problems, interrelated and powerful. The
first is the absence of anything even remotely similar in contemporary
English literature. The second is the presence of something similar in
contemporary Norwegian literature. I begin with the second.

Like *Eiríksmál*, *Haraldskvæði* is in mixed eddic meters and offers
dialogue between mythological creatures, specifically a valkyrie and a
raven. The transmission is problematic, but all three of the skalds whose
names are associated with the poem are Norwegian, and no evidence
links any of them with England. On the other hand, one of them, Þjóðólfr,
is linked to Sweden to some extent through his *Ynglingatal*.

Eiríksmál departs from *Haraldskvæði* by setting the poem in Valhǫll
and allowing Odin to speak, and these elements are the core of Kuhn's
argument. If, however, syncretism in the Danelaw was important to their
development, we may wonder at the ease with which the Norwegian
skald Eyvindr Skáldaspillir adapted those elements and developed them
for Eric's brother in *Hákonarmál*. Again, Hákon had spent much of his
childhood in England, but he returned to Norway as a young man. For
him there can be no question of Northumbrian syncretism. Syncretism
may easily have obtained around him, but it will have been of a specifically
English-Norwegian sort, and it is worth noting that he was on good terms
with the Hlaðir jarls. Indeed, most scholars (for example Marold and
Wolf) now read the conception of Valhǫll expressed in his memorial
poem as containing more archaic elements than those of *Eiríksmál*, but
only von See doubts the usual chronology, and his reversed chronology
does not seem to have won universal favor.

The three eddic "praise" poems (*Eiríksmál*, *Haraldskvæði*, and *Hákonarmál*) depart most significantly from skaldic style in their use of eddic
style. Eddic "mythology" poems rely on precisely those stylistic features
that set off the eddic praise poems: dialogue and mythological characters
and settings. What sets the three eddic praise poems off from other eddic
poems is the introduction of actual kings, well known to the audience—
and, for us, the transmission of poets' names with two of the texts.

Precisely these features are, however, also found in another poem
of Þjóðólfr, his *Ynglingatal*. It mentions a number of kings who increase
in historical authenticity as the poem progresses and finally reaches con-
temporaneity with Rǫgnvaldr Heiðumhæri. *Ynglingatal*'s connections,

however, are not with England and the Danelaw but rather with Sweden and Norway, and again, Eyvindr seems to have found little trouble in imitating the poem in his *Háleygjatal*. The larger context of *Eiríksmál*, then, seems to point away from England rather than toward it.

To return to the first of the interrelated problems: all three of the eddic praise poems contain material for which direct English parallels cannot be demonstrated. Indeed, the best evidence for English syncretism—given the lack of textual evidence—is offered by the stone carvings at Gosforth, and although Bailey (1980) identifies scenes of Ragnarǫk on the Gosforth cross, and Viðarr, Heimdallr, and Loki indeed appear almost certainly to be present, the scenes portray neither Odin the All-father nor the "new" Valhǫll; and locating Odin himself on any English carving is a very tricky business. Of the major gods, only Thor (Þórr) is reasonably certain, as the Gosforth "fishing-stone" seems unequivocally to show him fishing up the Midgard serpent. Precisely that subject was one of the most popular in the earliest skaldic poetry, which we must set in Norway. Thor and his opponent are also on the Altuna stone, and some scholars have put Bragi the Old, the first skald and one of those who sang of Thor's battle with Jǫrmungandr, in Sweden or even further east, thus reducing the specifically English connection. These poems and stones raise another question: if Odin rose to the status of all-father in England, why was Thor—as is generally accepted—the god most commonly worshipped there?

The parallels Kuhn thinks may be English are, in fact, not specifically English but generally Christian. Insofar as early Scandinavian Christianity came from England, we may look to English syncretism as a breeding ground for Norse mythology; but we must recall that Christianity reached Scandinavia through many conduits. The same objections apply to another argument based primarily on literary-historical evidence, namely, Wolfgang Butt's claim concerning the *Vǫluspá*. This argument is just as charged as those of Kuhn and just as important for the history of Scandinavian mythology; it, too, would sever the association between the language of *Vǫluspá* and the skalds of the Hlaðir jarls.

Butt's contribution appeared in 1969 and remains current because Joseph Harris cites it approvingly in two recent survey articles on eddic poetry (Harris 1984, 391; 1985, 94). It is significant because it offers a specific location for the composition of the *Vǫluspá*—the Danelaw—and a fairly specific date, 1001 to 1033. Butt's methodology is purely literary-historical; he believes that he has uncovered specific written sources for *Vǫluspá*. These are the homilies of Wulfstan and the poem *Judgment Day II*.

Let us examine the verbal similarities on which Butt bases his argument. The first examples are as follows:

Vǫluspá

Sal sá hon standa   sólo fiarri,
Nástrǫndo á,   norðr horfa dyrr;
fello eitrdropar   inn um lióra,
sá er undinn salr   orma hryggiom.

Sá hon þar vaða   þunga strauma
menn meinsvara   oc morðvarga,
oc þannz annars glepr   eyrarúno;
þar saug Níðhǫggr   nái framgengna,
sleit vargr vera—   vitoð er enn, eða hvat [st. 38–39]?

*   *   *

Sal sér hon standa   sólo fegra,
gulli þacþan,   á Gimlé;
þar scolo dyggvar   dróttir byggia
oc um aldrdaga   ynðis nióta [st. 64].

(She saw a hall stand   far from the sun,
on Nastrond,   its doors face north;
poison drops fell   in through the smoke-hole;
that hall is entwined   with the backs of snakes.

There she saw   wading through heavy streams
people who perjure   and murder-wargs,
and the one who seduces   another's true love.
There Nidhoggr sucked   the corpses of the dead,
the wolf tore people apart—   would you know more?

*   *   *

She saw a hall stand   fairer than the sun
thatched with gold,   at Gimle;
there shall righteous   peoples dwell
and forever   enjoy bliss.)

1. Wulfstan: *De regula canonicorum*

Not in the least are they manslaughterers nor traitors nor perjurers
nor murderers nor adulterers, but they maintain their rule always;
that is, their monastery. Not in the least are they liars, nor breakers
of pledges, nor robbers, nor plunderers, nor do they demand of
any people anything but what they wish people to ask of them
[Butt 192].

2. Wulfstan: *Sermo ad Anglos*

Here are manslaughterers and fratricides and murderers of priests
and persecutors of monasteries; here are perjurers and murderers,
and here are prostitutes and child-murderers and many fouly whoring fornicators; and here are wizards and witches; and here are

robbers and plunderers and despoilers, and—to say it most quickly—a countless number of all crimes and misdeeds
[Butt 273].

3. Wulfstan: *De fide catholica*

They shall henceforth go to hell with soul and with body and dwell among devils in the torments of hell. There fire is ever grimly recalled, there terror is eternal; there is deprivation and lamentation and perpetual sorrow everlastingly. Woe unto those who shall dwell there in agony. . . . Thither shall go manslaughterers, and thither shall go traitors; thither shall go adulterers and unclean fornicators; thither shall go perjurers and murderers; thither shall go misers, robbers, plunderers and despoilers; thither shall go thieves and criminals; thither shall go wizards and soothsayers, and—to say it most quickly—all the wicked who do evil and will not desist or be reconciled with God [Butt 162–63].

4. Wulfstan: *Sermo ad populum*

Thither shall go manslaughterers, and thither shall go perjurers; thither shall go adulterers and foul fornicators; thither shall go wizards and child-murderers. . .[Butt 231].

Butt believes that the two halls of *Vǫluspá* 38 and 64 belong together on the basis of the obvious verbal parallels. They reflect, then, the Christian heaven and hell, and a catalogue of sinners accompanies the picture of hell. The several parallel passages from Wulfstan's homilies also present a catalogue of sinners, though only in *Sermo ad populum* and perhaps in *De fide catholica* does Wulfstan introduce the motif in connection with a description of hell at the end of the world; and note, too, that *De regula canonicorum* was intended for a learned audience and therefore cannot itself be held to be a possible source of *Vǫluspá*. The three sorts of sinners in *Vǫluspá* 39 are to be found, Butt argues, among the many more sorts Wulfstan enumerates, and precise verbal echoes rule out, in his opinion, any possibility that the similarities are the result of chance. *Menn meinsvara* 'people who perjure' corresponds to *mansworan* 'perjurers' (Wulfstan texts 2–4); the poetic nonce-word *morðvargr* 'murder-warg, killer' imitates *mordwyrhta*, 'murder-doer, killer' (Wulfstan texts 1–3), arguably a term limited to Wulfstan; and the circumlocution of 39:5–6, "the one who seduces another's true love," is necessary because Norse has no suitable etymon for *æwbreca* 'adulterer' (Wulfstan texts 1 and 4).

To this we may begin with a textual objection. Even if we allow the juxtaposition of the halls in strophes 38 and 64, we are left in the *Codex Regius* version of the poem with two additional halls in strophe 37. These also share verbal parallels with strophes 38 and 64: *á Niðavǫllom, á Ókólni, á Gimlé* 'at Niðavellir, Ókolnir, Gimlé'; *Nástrǫndo á* 'on Nastrond'; *ór gulli* 'of gold'; *gulli þacþan* 'gold thatched'. In *Codex Regius,* the apparent association of all three halls with the "sinners" of strophe 39 (one for each hall?) makes less persuasive the equation of the halls of strophes 38 and 64.

Even if we are to disqualify strophe 37 for not occurring in both major manuscripts, I do not find the verbal parallels compelling. While it is true that nowhere is the adjective *meinsvarr attested in Norse, and that the related nouns (such as *meinsvari*) may be loans from Old English religious prose, the hypothetical Old English original is a noun, not an adjective. The compound is composed of perfectly good Norse components: compare *meinstafir* 'pernicious letters' in *Lokasenna* 28 and the term *eiðsvari* in *Þórsdrápa* 8. Finnur Jónsson (*Lexicon Poeticum* s.v.) reads *eiðsvari* as an adjective meaning 'those bound by oath' and the compound seems a direct antonym to *meinsvari*. Oaths were important in ancient Norse culture and particularly in myth and religion— note that the old sky god Týr finds his only role in the extant mythology in making good a bad oath, and that Ullr is primarily associated with oaths sworn on a certain ring—and I remain unconvinced that we need a concrete source to explain the appearance of the term in *Vǫluspá*.

The parallel between *mansworan* and *menn meinsvara* is, even so, the most compelling of the three alleged parallels. *Morðvargr* and *morðwyrhta* are simply not the same, although they look similar. The Norse word is a technical term in the legal language and refers to a true murderer (one who kills in secret). The Old English word has a similar meaning, but its associations, as Bethurum puts it, "are all with witchcraft" (1971, 310). An attempt to render *morðwyrhta* etymologically into Norse would yield *morð-yrkir*; the second component is unknown in literary Old Norse, although it may be attested in the dative singular on the eighth-century Eggjum rune stone. So much for the direct parallels. For "þann es annars eyraruno glepr," we are asked to postulate the model of Old English *æwbreca*. Even if we accept that the unclear Norse clause means 'adulterer' ("the one who seduces another's true love"), there is a difference in number—*æwbrecan* is plural, *þann* singular. Indeed, all the nouns in Wulfstan's catalogues are plural. If the *Vǫluspá* poet imitates a catalogue here, he does so in a highly idiosyncratic way.

Butt's argument is thus based on the general similarity of a catalogue of sinners (a beloved form in the Middle Ages), two questionable verbal parallels, and a possible translation. Butt argues that the juxtaposition of the catalogue of sinners with the end of the world is unusual, but that is hardly the case. One of the points of the judgment day is the punishment of the wicked, so sinners play a large role in Christian eschatology. Old English has, in fact, another poem with a short catalogue of sinners at the end of the world: *Christ III*, 1609–12a. Furthermore, as Wulfstan's style is in general based on cataloguing, it is hardly surprising that when the *Vǫluspá* poet falls into a catalogue, on a subject not dissimilar from Wulfstan's, the results should superficially resemble one another.

The *Vǫluspá* passage also contains material without parallel in

Wulfstan:

1. Hell and heaven as halls.
2. The place names Nástrǫnd and Gimlé and their attributes.
3. The notion that the doomed "wade through heavy streams."
4. Níðhǫggr sucking corpses and the wolf devouring men—apparently a typical Norse mythological collocation of wolf and serpent.

A basic problem seems to me to inform Butt's method. Once we accept that *Vǫluspá* reflects notions from Christianity, we may look everywhere, or so it seems to me, for specific models. Missionaries had been in Scandinavia for some time by the early eleventh century (Butt's dating of the text), and the millennium must have been on the minds of many.

As regards the halls, the first point above, we may note that iconography frequently or usually portrayed heaven as a building or even a town and used a gate or portico as its symbol and that vision literature often locates a hall or building in hell. Again I take an example from *Christ III*, in which hell is described in the context of the end of the world:

The house of torments is open and revealed, across from perjurers;
sinful people with black souls will fill it [1603b–06a].

A few lines later hell is called *morþerhusa mæst* 'greatest of murderhouses' (1624a) and *dreamleas hus* 'joyless house' (1627b). Here we may note in passing that iconography can have been involved in the postulated reformation of Valhǫll as a vast hall and that such iconography cannot be localized to Northumbria and England.

In vision literature, heaven and hell are usually separated by a river. Although it usually has a bridge over it—the narrow path of souls—there are visions in which sinners wade through the river. Boniface mentioned such a case in a letter of 717, and the German vision of Wethnus (*De visionibus Wethni*) repeats it. Níðhǫggr's sucking of corpses and the wolf's tearing of them are not so distant from the basic image of hell as devouring the souls of the evil; here note the iconographic feature of the maw of hell as a large monster's mouth, spitting flame and with great sharp teeth.

We now turn to Butt's other parallel passage:

Vǫluspá

Brœðr muno beriaz   oc at bǫnum verðaz,
muno systrungar   sifiom spilla;
hart er í heimi,   hórdómr mikill,
sceggǫld, scálmǫld,   scildir ro klofnir,
vindǫld, vargǫld,   áðr verold steypiz;
mun engi maðr   ǫðrom þyrma [45–46:1–2].

(Brothers will fight   and kill each other,
cousins will   commit adultery;

it is hard in the world,   much whoring,
an ax-age, a sword-age,   shields are split;
a wind-age, a wolf-age,   before the world falls;
no man will   spare another.)

Wulfstan: *Secundum Marcum*

No man is alive who may or can say how evil it will turn out
during that devilish time. At times brother will not spare brother,
nor father his child, nor child his own father, nor kin their kindred,
any more than strangers [Butt 140].

Butt stresses the moral or ethical quality of the two passages, a quality
he finds common in Old English but lacking in other Germanic literature
when kinsmen kill kinsmen; and he adds the philological observation that
the use of *spilla* 'kill', the compound *hórdómr* 'whoring', and the *annarr*
construction appear to have been influenced by Old English. In addition,
Vǫluspá 45:5–10 seems to Butt to display a general stylistic similarity to
the following passage from Wulfstan's *Secundum Marcum*—a kind of
breathless quality:

And nations will rage and struggle among themselves up to the
time when this shall take place. In addition there shall arise far
and wide conflict and injury, calumny and hatred and pillage,
battle and famine, fire and bloodshed and harsh disturbances,
plague and pestilence and a multitude of misfortunes [Butt 140].

We may pass over these alleged similarities; they are not compelling,
and indeed Butt makes little of them.

Neither is the parallel to *Vǫluspá* 45:1–4 convincing. The first question, if we accept Christian influence on these lines, is whether Wulfstan
offers the best possible model. The answer, of course, is no. The Old
High German *Muspilli* seems just as close: "dar ni mac denne mak an-
dremo helfan uora demo *Muspille*" ("there and then no kinsman can help
another, before that Muspilli"). Looking for specific analogues in Germanic languages, however, is unnecessary. If the ultimate source is Christian, one need look no further than the Bible. Mark 13:12 tells us that
"brother will deliver up brother to death, and the father his child, and
children will rise against parents and have them put to death." Wulfstan
was surely not the only person in northern Europe to paraphrase this
passage in a sermon.

The philological arguments are potentially persuasive, but customar-
ily subtle. Butt's reading of *spilla* as 'kill', a common usage of Old
English *spillan*, is based on Snorri's interpretation of the passage, which
may have been influenced by Mark 13:12.[2] Stefán Einarsson and Einar
Ól. Sveinsson argued in 1948 whether *hórdómr* was Norwegian or Icelandic, and Magnus Már Lárusson shows that there may be native usage at
work here, too. I am prepared to accept the *annarr* construction as a
possible sign of Old English influence, but it is only one phrase. There

is also ample philological evidence putting the poem far from the Danelaw; of the many examples, let me cite Hugo Pipping, who found arguments to locate the poem in Uppsala, whence it was, according to him, transported to Iceland by way of Hedeby and Norway.

Butt's third parallel is between numerous passages in *Vǫluspá* associated with Ragnarǫk and corresponding passages in *Judgment Day II*, an expanded translation of *De die judicii* by Bede or Alcuin, undertaken probably in the late tenth century.

Vǫluspá	*Judgment Day II*
Mountains crash together and witches fall. . .[52:5–6].	All the earth will tremble, and also the mountains will collapse and fall, and the sides of the mountains will buckle and melt,
The earth sinks into the sea. . .[57:2].	and the dreadful clamor of the rough sea will greatly trouble the hearts of all men.
The sunshine becomes black during the next summer, all weather woeful. . . [41:5–7].	In addition all the heaven will be black and obscured, greatly dimmed, dark and dim-hued, and black as chaos [99–105].
The sun turns black, the earth sinks into the sea, the bright stars vanish from heaven [57:1–4].	Then, without location, the stars will fall and the sun will grow dark immediately in the morning, nor will the moon have any whit of strength to put to flight the shadows of that night [107–10].
High heat licks against heaven itself. . . [57:7–8].	In addition, beyond all this all the upper air will be filled with poisonous flame. Fire will travel over all. . . [145–47a].
All are afraid on the road to Hel. . . [47:5–6].	There paupers and kings, impoverished and prosperous, all will be afraid; there will be one law for the wealthy and the poor, for they will feel terror all together.

... before Surt's kinsman
[i.e., Fenrir)
swallows that one [47:7–8].
There Níðhǫggr sucked
the corpses of the dead,
the wolf tore men. . .
                    [39:7–8].

That fierce flood
will flow rapidly with fire
and bitterly
consume the wretched souls,
and foul snakes
will cut and tear
the hearts
of those great sinners
                    [162–69].

And cruel
snakes will tear them
and gnaw their bones
with fiery teeth [211–12].

The sun knew not
where it had a hall,
the stars knew not
where their places were,
the moon knew not
what it had of strength
                    [5:5–10].

Then, without location,
the stars will fall,
and the sun will grow dark
immediately in the morning,
nor will the moon have
any whit of strength. . .
                    [107–09].

Judgment Day II is preserved only in Corpus Christi College, Cambridge, manuscript 201, a manuscript from Worcester or perhaps York containing important minor verse, some legal materials, the Old English Apollonius of Tyre, and homilies of Wulfstan. The manuscript evidence therefore places the poem in or near the Danelaw and associates it with Wulfstan. Butt believes that if the *Vǫluspá* poet did not know the poem itself, he had heard something like it in a sermon of Wulfstan.

Are the parallels compelling? Note that Butt has cut out sections of the Old English poem that bear no relationship to *Vǫluspá*, and that the order of events in *Judgment Day II* differs from that in *Vǫluspá*. Apocalypse was a popular subject in the Middle Ages, and one need not look far to find other verbal parallels to *Vǫluspá*.

The passages Butt singles out from *Vǫluspá* include the following motifs, in the order in which they appear in the Norse poem:

(1) *Vǫluspá* 5:5–10   chaos of heavenly bodies
(2) *Vǫluspá* 39:7–8   dragon and wolf devour corpses
(3) *Vǫluspá* 41:5–7   sun turns black, woeful weather
(4) *Vǫluspá* 47:5–6   all (men?) fear
(5) *Vǫluspá* 52:5-6   earthquake
(6) *Vǫluspá* 57:1–4   sun turns black; earth sinks into sea;
                         stars vanish
(7) *Vǫluspá* 57:7–8   flames lick the heavens.

We may dismiss at once the first parallel, as the chaos of heavenly bodies in *Vǫluspá* 5 occurs not at the end but at the beginning of the world.

The other motifs are omnipresent in apocalyptic tradition. Many of the motifs *Vǫluspá* assigns to Ragnarǫk are to be found in Revelation, not to mention the apocrypha. Revelation 6:12–17, for example, tells of an earthquake, the blackening of the sun and moon, the falling of the stars, the moving of mountains, and men's fear—an often stressed feature in apocalyptic literature. These catastrophes are repeated at various points in John's revelation, which also offers, in chapter 12, "one who is to rule all the nations," a clear analogue, as every student of *Vǫluspá* knows, to strophe 65(H). The chapter also offers the ubiquitous dragon of eschatological tradition, a beast that perhaps appears as one or more of *Vǫluspá's* dragons.

In Revelation and in Christian traditions of Judgment Day more generally, angels do battle with devils, a clear analogue to the last battle at Ragnarǫk. This motif is missing from *Judgment Day II*, which focuses on men's reactions to the end. *Vǫluspá* pays far less attention to that aspect of the story.

My complaint is more with Butt's method than with his conclusion. It seems impossible to me to pinpoint textual models for *Vǫluspá's* vision of the end, given the widespread popularity of apocalyptic traditions throughout the Middle Ages. If for other reasons the *Vǫluspá* poet may plausibly be located in the Danelaw ca. 1000, then he cannot have composed his poem beyond the bounds of the influence of Wulfstan's eschatological preaching and perhaps also of *Judgment Day II*. But if the poet's dates and location constitute the question, the alleged textual parallels cannot provide a convincing answer. He could have heard Wulfstan preaching about the Judgment Day—but he could have heard him in London, before 1002, and he might have heard another preacher, equally eloquent, in Norway or Iceland. *Íslendingabók*, *Hungrvaka*, and *Kristni saga* mention several bishops who were in Iceland around the millennium, and it is difficult to believe that they did not use conceptions of the Judgment Day either to impress their would-be converts or in sermons for the devout.

In searching for textual evidence, we may overlook other, less traceable evidence. Norsemen certainly saw iconography of the Judgment Day in many places, and presumably some of them learned what the images meant and contemplated the grand story that went with them. This could have happened anywhere, and the kind of syncretism in which *Vǫluspá* developed could just possibly have obtained only in a single poet's sensibility.

More generally, arguments of the sort Butt and Kuhn mount ignore the probability of a common pool of diction from which poets were free to choose. This is an extremely important methodological point. Unless we are certain that our manuscripts retain all that once existed, in oral or written form, we cannot estimate the size or extent of this pool, and we tread very thin ice in defending specific textual relationships. Lars

Lönnroth has argued this point in connection with one formula from the diction pool (1981, 323), and Joseph Harris (1985, 124–25) underlines the need for a whole new methodology in dealing with intertextual relationships among eddic poems. The argument goes beyond formulas, however, to any verbal similarities and is not limited to verse. Anyone who reads the Bible in connection with medieval eschatological literature cannot avoid it.

From my reading of these two scholars' methodology, I conclude that, on the basis of their arguments, we cannot prove at least part of what they set out to prove: the central importance of the geographical entity England, and particularly the Danelaw, in the formation of our extant Norse mythology. I would by no means deny England that importance, but I understand the process perhaps somewhat differently. What both Kuhn and Butt perceived was the influence of Christianity. I take it as a given that Norse mythology cannot be interpreted without reference to Christian influence, which may have been massive. This influence probably ranged from reforming old myths in Christian forms, probably by emphasizing certain aspects of the "original, pagan" myths, as Kuhn argued, through assimilation of Christian modes of expression, as Butt argued, to outright imitation of Christian forms. But seeking for specific geographic locations for the actual operation of this influence is almost certainly a lost cause. Christianity was by its nature an international religion, with a portable international language and portable culture. "Skaldic" culture, too, if I may use the term for the literary and religious culture of some Scandinavians during the ninth and tenth centuries, was also relatively portable. The two cultures had ample opportunities to meet and doubtless did so in an enormous number of contexts. A viking could perhaps be prime-signed in England, see Christian iconography in France, and have exempla retold to him while at sea. A priest might be born in England, educated in France, posted to Germany, and meet vikings in any of these places or at sea.

If we speak of English Christianity instead of Christianity in England, however, we are on the right track. Archaeological and textual evidence points increasingly to an important Christian presence in Norway during the tenth century, and the importance of the English church in Norway is well documented. The kind of syncretism Kuhn and Butt describe probably did obtain, but it can have obtained as easily in Norway as in England or been at work elsewhere in the Norwegian colonies or even further afield. What demands our attention is not where it took place, but how and why.

---

[1] A portion of this paper was delivered before the Old English Colloquium in Berkeley in 1983, and a draft of the entire paper was presented and discussed at the Sixth International Saga Conference in Helsingør in 1985. I am grateful to John McKinnell for his useful remarks, delivered as the official response to my paper at Helsingør, many of which have

found their way into this final version. All translations are my own.

2 "Muno systrungar sifiom spilla," literally "uterine cousins will destroy affinity, i.e., commit adultery." Butt argues that this usual translation is impossible (92). He proposes reading the line as Snorri paraphrases it: "and no one will spare his father in slayings or adultery" (*Gylfaginning* ch. 50) and notes that, if *spilla* means 'destroy' or 'kill' in *Vǫluspá*, its usage would accord with that of Old English.

WORKS CITED

Bailey, Richard N. *Viking Age Sculpture in Northern England.* London: Collins, 1980.

Bethurum, Dorothy, ed. *The Homilies of Wulfstan.* Oxford: Clarendon, 1957.

Boor, Helmut de. "Die religiöse Sprache der Vǫluspá." *Deutsche Islandforschung 1930.* Vol. 1: *Kultur.* Ed. Walther Heinrich Vogt. Breslau: F. Hirt, 1930. 68–142.

Bugge, Sophus. *Studier over de nordiske gude- og heltesagns oprindelse.* Vol. 1. Christiania: A. Cammermeyer, 1881–89.

_____. *Studien über die Entstehung der nordischen Götter und Heldensagen.* Trans. Oscar Brenner. Vol. 1. Munich: C. Kaiser, 1889.

Butt, Wolfgang. "Zur Herkunft der Vǫluspá." *Beiträge zur Geschichte der Deutschen Sprache und Literatur* 91 (1969): 83–103.

Einarsson, Stefán. "Eddu-smælki." *Skírnir* 122 (1948): 142–45.

Harris, Joseph. "Eddic Poetry." *Dictionary of the Middle Ages.* Gen. ed. Joseph Strayer. Vol. 4. New York: Scribner's, 1984. 385–92.

_____. "Eddic Poetry." *Old Norse-Icelandic Literature: A Critical Guide.* Ed. Carol J. Clover and John Lindow. Islandica 45. Ithaca: Cornell University Press, 1985. 68–156.

Helgason, Jón. "Höfuðlausnarhjal." *Einarsbók. Afmæliskveðja til Einars Ól. Sveinssonar.* 1969.

Kuhn, Hans. "Das nordgermanische Heidentum in den ersten christlichen Jahrhunderten." *Zeitschrift für deutsches Altertum* 79 (1942): 133–66. Rpt. in Kuhn, *Kleine Schriften* 2: 296–326.

_____. Review of Walter Baetke, *Die Götterlehre der Snorra-Edda. Anzeiger für deutsches Altertum* 65 (1952): 97–104. Rpt. in Kuhn, *Kleine Schriften* 2: 339–47.

_____. "Gaut." *Festschrift für Jost Trier zu seinem 60. Geburtstag am 15. Dezember 1954.* Meisenheim: A. Hain, 1954. 417–33. Rpt. in Kuhn, *Kleine Schriften* 2: 364–77.

_____. "Das Fortleben des germanischen Heidentums nach der Christianisierung." *La conversione al Cristianesimo nell'Europa dell'alto medioevo.* Settimane di studio del Centro italiano di studi sull'alto medioevo 14 (1967): 743–57. Rpt. in Kuhn, *Kleine Schriften* 2: 378–92.

_____. "Rund um die Vǫluspá." *Mediævalia litteraria: Festschrift für Helmut de Boor zum 80. Geburtstag.* Ed. Ursula Hennig and Herbert Kohl. Munich: C. H. Beck, 1971. 1–14.

_____. *Kleine Schriften.* 4 vols. Berlin: W. de Gruyter, 1969–78.

Láruson, Magnús Már. "Frændsemis- og sifjaspell." *Skírnir* 140 (1966): 128–42.

Lie, Hallvard. "Eiríksmál." *Kulturhistorikt lexicon för nordisk medeltid* 3: 536.

Lönnroth, Lars. "*Iǫrð fannz æva né upphiminn:* A formula analysis." *Specvlvm Norrœnvm: Norse Studies in Memory of Gabriel Turville-Petre.* Ed. Ursula Dronke et al. Odense: Odense University Press, 1981. 310–27.

Marold, Edith. "Das Walhallbild in den Eiríksmál und den Hákonarmál." *Mediaeval Scandinavia* 5 (1972): 19–33.

Munch, P. A., and C. R. Unger, eds. *Fagrskinna.* Christiania, 1847.

Nordal, Sigurður, ed. *Völuspá.* Reykjavik: Helgafell, 1923.

_____, ed. *Völuspá.* Trans. B. S. Benedikz and John McKinnell. Durham: Durham and St. Andrews Medieval Texts, 1978.

Pipping, Hugo. *Eddastudier II.* Studier i nordisk filologi 17, 3; Skrifter utgivna av Svenska Litteratursällskapet i Finland 189. Helsingfors, 1928.

Schier, Kurt. "Zur Mythologie der *Snorra Edda.*" *Specvlvm Norrœnvm: Norse Studies in*

Memory of Gabriel Turville-Petre. Ed. Ursula Dronke et al. Odense: Odense University Press, 1983. 405–20.

See, Klaus von. "Zwei eddische Preislieder: Eiríksmál und Hákonarmál." *Festgabe für Ulrich Pretzel zum 65. Geburtstag dargebracht von Freunden und Schülern*. Ed. Werner Simon et al. Berlin: E. Schmidt, 1963. 107–17.

Sveinsson, Einar Ól. "Lítil athugasemd." *Skírnir* 122 (1948): 146–51.

Wolf, Alois. "Zitat und Polemik in den 'Hákonarmál' Eyvinds." *Germanistische Studien*. Ed. Johannes Erben and Eugen Thurnher. Innsbrucker Beiträge zur Kulturwissenschaft 15. Innsbruck: Institut für vergleichende Sprachwissenschaft der Universität Innsbruck, 1969. 9–32.

NORSE MYTHOLOGY AND NORTHUMBRIA: A RESPONSE

JOHN MCKINNELL
University of Durham

WHEN JOHN LINDOW presented his foregoing paper at the Sixth International Saga Conference at Helsingør in July 1985, I did not, as respondent, find very much in it with which to disagree. Now that it has been revised and most of the comments made then have been taken into consideration, there remain no significant differences of view between us. I shall therefore confine this response to looking at the syncretism to be found in one small section of *Vǫluspá* and comparing it with the views deducible from tenth-century Northumbrian sculpture in which heathen mythological subjects appear.[1]

I

Wolfgang Butt's argument in favor of *Vǫluspá* having identifiable English sources begins with the contention that stanzas 38 and 64 "belong together." He argues as follows (Butt 85–87, especially footnote 12):

1. There are close verbal parallels between the two stanzas.
2. It appears from chapter 52 of *Gylfaginning*, in which the contents of stanzas 37 and 64 of *Vǫluspá* are used together immediately before quotation of stanzas 38 and 39 (lines 1–4), that Snorri was using a text of *Vǫluspá* in which these stanzas all occurred together after the description of Ragnarǫk. The order of stanzas in *Hauksbók* is then regarded as intermediate between those in *Codex Regius* and in the lost manuscript used by Snorri.
3. Butt debates whether the order of stanzas in *Codex Regius* or the one supposedly inherited by Snorri is the original without reaching a firm conclusion either way.

One may accept the first of these arguments without being impressed by the other two. The verbal parallels between stanzas 38 and 64 do have the obvious function of contrasting the ultimate fates of the wicked and the virtuous (or, more exactly, the treacherous and the reliable); but the two groups need not encounter their rewards at the same fictional time or in the same part of the poem.

The assumption that Snorri used the stanzas of *Vǫluspá* in the exact order in which they stood in his received text cannot be supported. For example, stanza 52 (on Ragnarǫk) is quoted in *Gylfaginning* chapter 4 almost immediately after stanza 3 (on the beginning of the world); the substance of stanzas 17–18 (on the first human beings) appears in chapter 9; then stanzas 40–41 (on Fenrir's children) are quoted in chapter 12 before he reverts in chapter 14 to the description of the golden age and the dwarves, the substance of *Vǫluspá* stanzas 7–16; and the next stanzas quoted are then stanza 28 (on the *vǫlva* herself) in chapter 15, stanza 19 (on Yggdrasill) in chapter 16, and stanza 64 (on the rewards of the virtuous) in chapter 17. Without Snorri's accompanying prose, this order of stanzas would not form any logical sequence. The use of stanza 64 in chapter 17 as well as in chapter 52 is particularly embarrassing for Butt's argument, since it is one of the stanzas with which he is immediately concerned and shows that Snorri was quite capable of using the same stanza more than once.

Nor does comparison with the order in *Hauksbók* provide any support for Butt's view. Snorri's text of the stanzas he quotes from *Vǫluspá* often does agree with *Hauksbók* in textual details, but, although the order in *Hauksbók* differs markedly from that in *Codex Regius* between stanzas 21 and 44 (for the *Hauksbók* order, see Nordal 1978, 42), *Gylfaginning* does not follow it in any respect, nor could it, since the *Hauksbók* order is often nonsensical. For example, it places stanzas 25–26 (the encounter with the giant builder) long before stanza 24 (the destruction of the wall that makes the employment of the giant builder necessary); and the punishment of Loki in stanzas 34–35 immediately follows the war with the Vanir in stanzas 23–24, whereas the murder of Baldr, which is the cause for Loki's punishment, is left out altogether.

The order of stanzas used in *Gylfaginning* seems, therefore, to be due principally to Snorri's own structural design, not to the hypothetical order of stanzas in some lost *Vǫluspá* manuscript used by him; and in the work of a thirteenth-century Christian it is no surprise that the punishment of the wicked and the reward of the virtuous should be brought together, no matter where they stood in the manuscript he inherited.

When we turn to the last part of Butt's argument, he seems right to suggest that a "Christianizing" of a stanza order that originally diverged from Christian ideas is more probable than the reverse. But his counter arguments are less convincing. As Lindow shows, there is no need to suppose direct influence from Wulfstan on *Vǫluspá*, so that his argument based on a single verbal coincidence between them has no force. Nor is it necessary to move stanzas 38–39 of *Vǫluspá* to a position after stanza 64 in order to explain the apparent return of evil in stanza 66. This return can be accounted for either by proposing that the poet held a cyclical view of the world (see Schjødt) or, perhaps better, by regarding stanza 66 as a return to the framework of the poem and thus as taking place at the same fictional time as stanzas 1 and 28–29. The flying dragon of stanza 66 would then be the first symptom that the future just prophesied by the *vǫlva* is beginning to come about.

This is not, of course, to deny that the concept of reward or punishment after death in stanzas 38–39 and 64 of *Vǫluspá* is influenced by Christian thought. But to demonstrate syncretic use of Christian values, we must rather seek to show how they are used in separate parts of a heathen work than to try to lump them together. It is easy enough to see how the reward of reliable men in stanza 64 fits into the idealized reborn world of the end of the poem, but the context of stanzas 38–39 requires more elucidation.

Stanzas 31–35 are concerned with the slaying of Baldr and the vengeance taken for it in the killing of Hǫðr and the binding of Loki. This vengeance represents a vigorous, but ultimately vain, attempt by the Æsir to punish and deter treachery, and it is perhaps in this light that the punishment of human treachery (the subject of stanzas 38–39) should also be seen. In this poem, Loki is consistently the master of deceit; it is he who has mingled the sky with deceit (*lævi*, 25.6), and the only adjective applied to him is *lægjarn* 'fond of deceit' (35.3). It is appropriate that treacherous men should be punished at the same time as he is.

The most obvious Biblical parallel to this is in Revelation 20–21, in which Satan is bound for a thousand years "that he should deceive the nations no more" (20.3). He is then freed and gathers to battle those he has deceived (20.7–8), but they are devoured with fire from heaven and cast into an everlasting lake of fire (20.9–10), where they are joined by all whose names are not written in the book of life (i.e., the wicked, 20.15, 21.8). The resemblances between this and Loki's career in *Vǫluspá* are obvious; the only discrepancy is that the punishment of the treacherous in the poem is associated with the binding of Loki rather than with what happens after Ragnarǫk. But as the fire in *Vǫluspá* is seen realistically as a means of destruction rather than symbolically as flames of torment, Loki does not survive after Ragnarǫk to remain the paradigm of the wicked, so that change was unavoidable.

It is hard to say how much of this account was imported into Norse by the *Vǫluspá* poet or his predecessors and how much was already paralleled in native mythology before Christian influence became important. But the punishment of the wicked, at least, must be due to direct Christian influence. The most probable ultimate source for it (no doubt as modulated through preaching) is Revelation 21.8:

> Timidis autem, et incredulis, et exsecratis, et homicidis,
> et fornicatoribus, et veneficis, et idololatris, et
> omnibus mendacibus, pars illorum erit in stagno ardenti

igne et sulphure: quod est mors secunda.

(But the fearful, and unbelieving, and the abominable,
and murderers, and whoremongers, and sorcerers, and
idolators and all liars, shall have their part in the
lake which burneth with fire and brimstone: which is the
second death.)

Not all of these types of sin would mean much to a heathen of the Viking
Age, but the three categories of ill-doer that appear in Vǫluspá (st. 39)—
oathbreakers (i.e., "all liars"), murderers, and seducers— are all here.
Norse ethics being what they were, it may surprise us that cowards and
sorcerers are not included in the poem's list as well. But the frightened
have their own dishonored place in Vǫluspá, on the roads to Hel (47.5–6),
and although sorcery was disapproved of and seiðr 'magic' was seen as
being practiced by wicked women (22.7–8), it would be strange and
perhaps artistically tactless for the vǫlva, a sorceress herself, to have
reveled in their inclusion in such a punishment.

The poet therefore seems to be making a personal selection from
the Christian material. But the poet may be doing so with a further ironic
purpose, since oathbreaking and murder, two of the three types of crime
punished in stanza 39, are things of which the Æsir are collectively guilty
themselves, in the killing of the giant builder (st. 26). The third, seduction,
cannot now be seen in their behavior in Vǫluspá, but this could be
explained in either of two ways. This couplet (39.5–6) is not quoted by
Snorri, though he does include the other two crimes, and it seems to be
based on stanza 115 of Hávamál or on a proverb also used there. As the
stanza has ten half-lines rather than the usual eight, this couplet may not
be original to the poem. Alternatively, the link with Hávamál may imply
a seduction by Óðinn to which there is or was an allusion earlier in the
poem that we cannot now recognize, one perhaps in the Gullveig story
or in the origins of the war with the Vanir. That he is capable of such
seductions is clear from the Gunnlǫð episode in Hávamál (st. 102–10).

The result of this double standard on the part of the Æsir is to
disqualify them as impartial judges and to reduce their "justice," in the
punishment of Loki, to the level of mere feud. It is therefore no surprise
that stanza 40 of Vǫluspá shows us Loki's kindred preparing for the
revenge that will reach its fulfillment in Ragnarǫk.

But this interpretation omits stanza 37. This is used in chapter 52
of Gylfaginning, and although it is not in Hauksbók, it need not therefore
be interpolated, for Hauksbók also omits stanzas 28–33 and 36, and all
of these except 30 (the list of valkyries) are essential to the narrative
structure of the poem. But there are other problems about accepting stanza
37 as original in its present position. Its two halls both have pleasant
connotations that seem unsuitable in places of punishment—one is a salr
ór gulli 'hall of gold' and the other a bjórsalr 'beer hall'—and they are

apparently under the control of giants, and so are not part of the gods' attempt to deter evil in the world. There is certainly no need to suggest (as Lindow does) that each hall is to be associated with one category of sinner.

If stanza 37 is removed, a vivid cumulative image comes into focus. The deadly River Slíðr of stanza 36 is followed by the description of the hall woven (like wattle?) with snakes whose poison drops on those inside, just as another snake drops its venom on Loki (a detail clearly implied by the presence of Sigyn in stanza 35). It is "there," i.e., inside the hall (39.1), that the treacherous must wade the grievous current, and this image of a swiftly flowing river rushing through a hall is also familiar as an omen of disaster in dreams and visions (see *Atlamál* st. 24, Dronke 81; *Heiðarvíga saga* ch. 26, Nordal and Jónsson 290; Turville-Petre 1972, 47–48). But this image is disrupted in *Codex Regius* by the cheerful halls of stanza 37. This may suggest either that stanza 37 has been interpolated because of the mention of a hall in stanza 38, as suggested by Finnur Jónsson, or that it is part of the description of the gods' enemies and properly belongs before stanza 40, as implied by Boer (Nordal 1978, 76 and references). The latter idea is attractive, because the link between the dismal hall of torture, presumably ordained by the gods, and the cheerful halls of their foes would help to unify the poem and underline the fallen state of the gods. Either suggestion would clarify the sequence of thought, but whether or not that is sufficient reason for moving or removing stanza 37 must remain a matter of opinion.

In any event, this section of *Vǫluspá* does employ genuine syncretism—that is, it uses individual Christian images and ideas as part of an overall view that is not the standard Christian one. The geographical source of this syncretism is another and much more difficult matter, for Wulfstan can certainly not have been the only preacher of his day to use this passage from Revelation (which, we may note in passing, is itself somewhat closer to the categories of sinner in *Vǫluspá* than are any of the elaborations of it by Wulfstan with which Butt makes comparison). The next question is whether or not a similar syncretism can be seen in Northumbria at the same period, and some clue to its answer may be derived from the rather small body of Northumbrian sculpture that depicts (or may depict) heathen mythological subjects.

II

It must be stressed that most Viking Age sculpture from Northern England is unambiguously Christian, and even if we accept all the possible identifications discussed below, mythological subjects are rather rare. Yorkshire and Cleveland, for example, have over five hundred surviving pieces of sculpture, of which only four deserve even a mention here.

The commonest are mythological scenes depicting some aspect of

Ragnarǫk. Two sculptures may give general views of it, though both identifications are uncertain; they are on the Skipwith stone (North Yorkshire: Bailey 1980, plate 38) and the second side of the Sockburn hogback (Co. Durham: Bailey 1980, 135, fig. 26; Cramp 1984, pt. 2, 767–68, plate 46). In the latter, Fenrir seems to be the most important character, since the other side of the stone shows what may be his binding. An alternative explanation of this scene, that it represents Daniel in the lions' den (Cramp 1984, pt. 1, 143–44,) would involve a contrast between Christian and heathen scenes on opposite sides of the stone, a collocation which is quite possible.

Heimdallr, depicted at or just before Ragnarǫk, probably appears on the Gosforth cross (Cumbria: Bailey 1980, 126, fig. 23), where he seems to be "labeled" by the horn he carries and is shown fending off two serpentine monsters with a spear or staff. Since Heimdallr is said by Snorri to be destined to fight Loki at Ragnarǫk (*Gylfaginning* ch. 51, Faulkes 51), this suggests either that the Gosforth sculptor knew the story in a different form, one in which Heimdallr fought at least two (serpentine?) monsters or, perhaps more likely, that these monsters are a generalization of all the gods' opponents, against whom Heimdallr acts as watchman. A cross fragment at Ovingham (Northumberland: Bailey 1980, 134, fig. 24) also depicts a man with what seems to be a large horn—most likely Heimdallr (since Víðarr and Fenrir probably appear on the same panel) although the possibility has been suggested that the figure may be Goliath with a club.

There are two probable depictions of Víðarr. The better known, on the Gosforth cross, seems to show him forcing the jaws of a monster apart, as described in stanza 53 of *Vafþrúðnismál*. The problem here, that the monster looks like a serpent rather than a wolf, may be disregarded if the Gosforth sculptor is thought to have depicted all the gods' enemies at Ragnarǫk in this symbolic fashion, as with the figure of Heimdallr discussed above; alternatively, the man in this scene could be Þórr rather than Víðarr, in which case the monster would be the World Serpent, and the detail of its jaws being forced apart might have been borrowed from the Víðarr story. (That details of Þórr's exploits at Ragnarǫk could vary is shown by *Hymiskviða* stanza 11, in which he is called *Hróðrs andskoti* 'opponent of the Wolf'.) The other probable appearance of Víðarr is on the Ovingham cross-fragment, where the human figure on the left is wrestling with a monster that strains upwards towards a disk that Bailey argues is a conventional representation of the sun (1980, 133). If this supposition is correct, the monster (which is very indistinct in detail but has legs and is more like a wolf than a serpent) must be Fenrir, which will devour the sun (*Vafþrúðnismál* st. 46–47), and the man fighting him is probably Víðarr. Alternatively, the three figures on the Ovingham panel could be David, his lion, and Goliath (Cramp 1984, pt. 1, 215–16; pt. 2, 1199, plate 210), but this explanation seems unlikely; it leaves the disk unexplained and conflicts with the Biblical account, according to which Goliath's weapons were dagger, spear, and sword (1 Samuel 17.6–7, 51).

Two other scenes occur, once each, because of their narrative links to Ragnarǫk. On the Gosforth cross there is a bound Loki, with his wife Sigyn kneeling over him with a bowl in which to catch the venom from a serpent hanging above him, as described in stanza 35 of *Vǫluspá* and chapter 50 of *Gylfaginning* (Faulkes 49). But Loki is "the Wolf's father" (*Lokasenna* st. 10), and his breaking free will signal the beginning of Ragnarǫk, so a scene depicting him bound is an appropriate part of the decorative scheme of a cross whose main heathen image is Ragnarǫk (Bailey 1980, 128–29). Another carving that has been interpreted as showing the bound Loki is the so-called "Bound Devil" in Kirkby Stephen church, Cumbria (Bailey 1980, 138–40, plate 40), but I agree with Bailey in rejecting this identification. The iconography has nothing in common with that on the Gosforth cross nor with such pictures of the bound Satan as those in the manuscript of Junius 11 (pp. 3, 16, 17, 20, 36), all of which depict the victim from the side rather than straight on, as at Kirkby Stephen. It does, however, show a strong resemblance to the Yorkshire Vǫlundr carvings, especially to that on the Leeds cross (Bailey 1980, 105), and may perhaps be best interpreted as a misunderstanding of Vǫlundr figures that the carver had seen.

The other subject linked to Ragnarǫk thematically is the binding of Fenrir and Týr's loss of his hand, which may be the subject of the first side of the Sockburn hogback discussed above. Like the bound Loki at Gosforth, this subject is best seen as a prologue to the probable Ragnarǫk scene on the other side of the same stone. It might be significant that the stories of Loki and Fenrir are both concerned with the binding of a demon, like that of Satan in Revelation 20, but since the Gosforth cross is a Christian monument and the identification of the subject on the Sockburn hogback is uncertain, it would be unwise to make too much of this correspondence.

Mythological subjects unconnected with Ragnarǫk are few and, with one exception, doubtful. The one certain subject is Þórr fishing for the World Serpent, the subject of the lower of the two scenes on the Gosforth "Fishing Stone" (Cumbria: Bailey 1980, 131–32, plate 36). In this case, it seems that comparison is being made between the fighting of serpentine representatives of evil by Þórr and by Christ.

Four or five stones might be thought to depict Óðinn. The fragmentary cross from Kirkbymoorside (North Yorkshire: Bailey 1980, 134, fig. 25) shows what may be a hanged man, possibly Óðinn. But this identification is very doubtful. The object round the man's neck is not certainly a rope, and there are no other surviving figures on the stone with which comparison might be made. Nor does the iconography of the figure, seen straight on, resemble the hanged Óðinn on the Gotlandic stone Stora

Lärbro Hammars I, who is seen side on, is hanged on a fairly naturalistic
tree, and is carrying a shield (Lindqvist 1: fig. 81; 2: 86–87, figs. 429,
440), though this lack of resemblance does not, of course, prove that the
former figure cannot be Óðinn.

On three or four stones, Óðinn may be "labeled" by a bird or birds
on his shoulder(s), as he certainly is on the Kirk Andreas cross, Isle of
Man (Turville-Petre 1964, plate 38; Cubbon 32). At the foot of the north
face of the Leeds cross (West Yorkshire: Bailey 1980, plate 4) there is
a figure brandishing a sword, with a bird on his left shoulder and what
looks like a triquetra in the bottom left-hand corner of the panel—a
symbol used to "label" Óðinn on a number of Gotlandic picture stones
(e.g., Alskog Tjängvide I, Lärbro Hammars I, Lärbro Tängelgärde I,
Lindqvist 1: figs. 137, 81, 86, Lindqvist 2: 15–17, 86–87, 92–93, figs.
305, 429, 448). A non-Christian figure would not be unexpected in this
position, for the same panel on the south face is occupied by a Vǫlundr
scene (Bailey 1980, plate 29). The only figure above the man with the
bird seems to be a cherub, while above the Vǫlundr figure is a full-length
figure, possibly a larger angel. Both faces may represent contrasts on the
theme of flying between old heroic or mythological stories and their
Christian counterparts. If so, the raven as Óðinn's messenger is being
compared, probably unfavorably, with the cherub. Another interpretation
would identify the Leeds figure with an earlier stage of the Vǫlundr story,
in which case the "triquetra" would be reinterpreted as an anvil (Lang
1976, 91–92), but this theory is rendered less likely by the absence of
other Vǫlundr figures with this iconography and the lack of a thematic
link with the cherub above. A third possibility, that it is St. John the
Evangelist, would see the "sword" as a quill pen and the "triquetra" as
a small table. This otherwise attractive interpretation is probably to be
ruled out because Lang has tentatively identified this same subject at the
top of the south face of the cross; it seems unlikely that the same subject
would be carved twice on one cross.

There is also a figure with birds on both shoulders on the fragmentary
cross-shaft from Kirkleavington (Cleveland: Bailey 1980, plate 57), but
its iconography has nothing in common with that on the Leeds cross,
and there is nothing else to suggest identification with Óðinn. Another
figure probably of the same type, though now much faded, can be seen
on Billingham stone I (Co. Durham: Cramp 1984, pt. 1, 48; pt. 2, 69,
plate 15), and it is possible that the now fragmentary Billingham stone
12 (Cramp 1984, pt. 1, 51; pt. 2, 83, plate 17) had the same iconography.
Billingham and Kirkleavington are only about ten miles apart. These
figures could be secular portraits (see Cramp and Lang no. 12), but it is
more probable that they are of Christian significance. Parallels to them
can be found in a miniature of Christ, of the eighth or ninth century and
probably from western Germany (in MS. Vat. Pal. 220, fol. 1r [Saxl
11–13]), and in a tomb mosaic from Tabarca, Tunisia, of the late fourth

or early fifth century, which may depict the man commemorated, one Crescentius, and shows a man dressed as a priest (Du Bourguet 158).

Bailey also suggests that both the complete and the fragmentary hogback from Lowther (Cumbria: Bailey 1980, 136–38; see plate 35 and fig. 27 for the complete stone, fig. 29 for the fragment) may embody a single heathen iconography. He suggests that the continuous looped serpent that runs along the bottom of all the Lowther carvings (which has a head on the fragment and on the first side of the complete stone and probably a tail on the second side of the complete stone) is the World Serpent, but proposes no meaning for the scenes as a whole. The first side of the complete hogback shows two groups of warriors with shields; those on the left are on a ship, with a fish under it to indicate the sea, while those on the right appear to be on land. Between them, facing forwards, is a large seated (?) figure, probably female. This scene also appears on two Gotlandic stones (Stenkyrka Smiss I [Lindqvist 1: fig. 97; 2: 128–29 and figs. 521, 523] and Lärbro Hammars I [Lindqvist 1: fig. 81; 2: 86–87 and fig. 429]), except that there the female figure is standing and faces the ship-borne warriors. The second side of the Lowther stone shows six women, visible only from the waist upwards, with prominent and highly stylized hair, curled outwards at the ends, and this motif is repeated in a more stiff and angular way on the surviving face of the fragmentary hogback, where four women can be seen on what remains. I do not know of any Gotlandic parallels to this scene.

Stanza 14 of *Grímnismál* tells us that Freyja chooses half the slain every day, while Óðinn takes the other half. But the Vanir, of whom Freyja is the chief female representative, are particularly gods of the sea (Turville-Petre 1964, 163–64, 178). It seems possible that Freyja's half of the slain are those who die at sea, those in the ship on the Lowther, Stenkyrka Smiss, and Lärbro Hammars stones. If so, this scene becomes a nautical equivalent to the scene, so common on Gotlandic stones, in which the dead warrior is received at Valhǫll by a woman (presumably a valkyrie) bearing a drinking horn. It would then be possible to interpret the women on the second side of the complete Lowther hogback as waves, personified as the daughters of Ægir and Rán (see *Helgakviða Hundingsbana I* st. 29; *Skáldskaparmál* chs. 23, 31, 58; ed. Finnur Jónsson 92, 96–97, 135). Although Snorri gives nine daughters of Rán rather than six, the multiple of three is probably more important than the actual number. Such an interpretation must be very tentative, but it would explain why these figures can be seen only from the waist upwards, and why their hair is so stylized and wave-like. It must be admitted, though, that it suits the flowing curves of the complete hogback better than the solid figures of the fragment. If this interpretation were correct, the Lowther hogbacks might commemorate men (or a single man) who had died at sea. But whatever their meaning, the parallel with the iconography of the two Gotlandic stones suggests a pagan rather than a Christian interpretation.

Another monument which may be related to the Lowther hogbacks is the so-called "Warrior's Tomb" hogback at Gosforth (Bailey 1980, plate 23; Collingwood 172–73), which also shows two groups of warriors. Collingwood's drawing shows, between the two groups, a kneeling figure facing left, but this figure is not clear in the photograph published by Bailey—one that is less than ideal, however, and taken from an oblique angle. No sign of a ship survives, but the bottom of the panel is damaged. The other side of the stone shows a nonfigurative plait and thus gives no help towards the interpretation of this scene, which might be another version of the "division of the slain" motif (if that is what is depicted at Lowther) but cannot be convincingly identified.

A few conclusions seem possible. First, sculpture alluding to heathen mythology is rare in Northern England and is concentrated at very few sites, the most important of which, Gosforth, may have had some links with the Hiberno-Norse culture of the Isle of Man; compare, for example, the Heimdallr figure on the Jurby cross-slab (Cubbon 31).

Second, where heathen mythology is or may be alluded to, scenes connected in some way with Ragnarǫk are commoner than any others, though Þórr's fishing for the World Serpent also appears, and there may (more doubtfully) be representations of Óðinn, Freyja, and the daughters of Ægir. A common concern with Ragnarǫk may appear to link *Vǫluspá* and the Northumbrian sculpture, and this may be due to the influence of Christian millenarianism on both. Even if the Gosforth cross is dated to the mid- rather than the late tenth century, the millenarian idea may already have been powerful by then; but this influence was so powerful throughout northern Europe in the tenth and early eleventh centuries (Nordal 1970–71, 113–18) that it would be a mistake to regard it as a specifically Northumbrian influence on *Vǫluspá*.

Finally, on the three monuments where Christian and heathen iconography occur together (the Gosforth cross, the Gosforth "Fishing Stone," and probably the Leeds cross), the heathen iconography is clearly used for a wholly Christian purpose. The Gosforth cross demonstrates the inability of the old gods to conquer at Ragnarǫk as Christ conquered on the Cross; the Fishing Stone shows Christ as the hart overcoming the serpent Satan, while Þórr (in most versions of the story, see Turville-Petre 1964, 75–76) is unable to do likewise. The Leeds cross may compare Óðinn's raven unfavorably with God's cherub. This is not a syncretic use of Christian material to contribute to a heathen view, as in *Vǫluspá*, but something quite different: an exemplary use of heathen material to enforce a predetermined Christian message. The same probably applies even to those monuments for which the sculptor's understanding of Christianity may have been imperfect, such as the strange skull-headed cross-slab from York Minster (Bailey 1980, plate 6, left hand slab), which may be intended to show the dead Christ on the Cross.

Most of the other monuments discussed here either are probably not concerned with heathen myth at all (Kirkby Stephen, Kirkleavington, Billingham) or else are too fragmentary for any conclusions about the purpose of their heathen or possibly heathen iconography to be possible (Kirkbymoorside, Ovingham, Skipwith). It has even been suggested recently that all the non-Christian stones should be regarded as secular rather than pagan (Bailey 1985, 60–61), but while this certainly seems a sound view of carvings depicting legendary heroes like Sigurðr (e.g., the Halton cross, Bailey 1980, 120 and fig. 15) or Vǫlundr (e.g., the Leeds cross), the monuments discussed in this article are those that allude to systems of belief, especially about death and the end of the world. Whether such stones indicate genuine religious belief or merely represent an antiquarian interest and pleasure in the old myths is a question that cannot now be answered. But in either case, they must be regarded as heathen in some sense, except where they are or may have been juxtaposed with, and subordinated to, images of Christian origin. On this basis, the only truly heathen monuments are the hogbacks from Lowther and Sockburn, and perhaps the "Warrior's Tomb" at Gosforth; but these stones show no Christian influence at all, unless we regard the second side of the Sockburn stone as depicting Daniel rather than Ragnarǫk, in which case Daniel's prefiguring of Christ would be contrasted with the ultimate failure of Týr's binding of Fenrir, and this monument, too, would be designed to show the superiority of the new religion to the old. In either case, real syncretism is absent.

None of these conclusions, of course, demonstrates that Vǫluspá cannot have been composed in Northumbria, but there is no evidence for such an origin that might counter suggestions of composition elsewhere (Nordal 1970–71, 111–13); and the Northumbrian sculpture, for what the present observation is worth, does not appear to show any genuine syncretism of the type found in Vǫluspá.

I should like to acknowledge the helpful suggestions made to me by Professor Richard Bailey during the preparation of this paper.

WORKS CITED

Bailey, Richard N. "Aspects of Viking-Age Sculpture in Cumbria." *The Scandinavians in Cumbria*. Ed. J. R. Baldwin and I. D. Whyte. Edinburgh: Scottish Society for Northern Studies, 1985. 52–63.

_____. *Viking Age Sculpture in Northern England*. London: Collins, 1980.

Biblia Sacra iuxta Vulgatam Clementinam, Nova Editio. Madrid: Biblioteca de Autores Cristianos, 1965. (Translations from the Authorised Version.)

Butt, Wolfgang. "Zur Herkunft des Vǫluspá." *Beiträge zur Geschichte der deutschen Sprache und Literatur* 91 (1964): 82–103.

Collingwood, W. G. *Northumbrian Crosses of the pre-Norman Age*. London: Faber and Gwyer, 1927.

Cramp, Rosemary J. *Corpus of Anglo-Saxon Stone Sculpture in England, I: County Durham and Northumberland*. 2 parts. Oxford: British Academy, 1984.

Cramp, Rosemary J. and James T. Lang. *A Century of Anglo-Saxon Sculpture*. Newcastle-upon-Tyne: Frank Graham, 1977.

Cubbon, A. M. *The Art of the Manx Crosses*. 2nd ed. Douglas: The Manx Museum and National Trust, 1977.

Dronke, Ursula, ed. *The Poetic Edda: Vol. 1: Heroic Poems*. Oxford: Clarendon, 1969.

Du Bourguet, P. *Early Christian Painting*. Trans. S. W. Taylor. New York: Viking, 1965.

Gollancz, Sir Israel, ed. *The Cædmon Manuscript of Anglo-Saxon Biblical Poetry: Junius XI in the Bodleian Library*. Oxford: Clarendon, 1927.

Lang, James T. "Sigurd and Weland in Pre-Conquest Carving from Northern England." *Yorkshire Archaeological Journal* 48 (1976): 83–94.

_____. "Anglo-Scandinavian Sculpture in Yorkshire." *Viking York and the North*. Ed. R. A. Hall. C.B.A. Research Report 27 (1978): 11–19.

Lindqvist, Sune. *Gotlands Bildesteine*. 2 vols. Stockholm: Kungliga Vitterhets Historie och Antikvitetsakademie, 1941–42.

Neckel, Gustav, ed. *Edda. Vol. 1: Text*. 3rd ed. rev. by Hans Kuhn. Heidelberg: Winter, 1962.

Nordal, Sigurður. "Three Essays on Vǫluspá." Trans. B. S. Benedikz and John McKinnell. *Saga-Book* 18 (1970–71): 79–135.

_____, ed. *Vǫluspá*. Trans. B. S. Benedikz and John McKinnell. Durham: Durham and St. Andrews Medieval Texts, 1978.

Nordal, Sigurður, and Guðni Jónsson, eds. *Borgfirðinga sögur. Íslenzk fornrit*. Vol. 3. Reykjavik: Hið íslenzka fornritafélag, 1938.

Saxl, F. "The Ruthwell Cross." *Journal of the Warburg and Courtauld Institutes* 6 (1943): 1–19.

Schjødt, Jens Peter. "*Vǫluspá*: Cyclisk tidsopfattelse i gammelnordisk religion." *Danske Studier* 76 (1981): 91–95.

Sturluson, Snorri. *Edda*. Ed. Finnur Jónsson. Copenhagen: G. E. C. Gad, 1900.

_____. *Edda, Prologue and Gylfaginning*. Ed. A. Faulkes. Oxford: Clarendon, 1982.

Turville-Petre, E. O. G. *Myth and Religion of the North*. London: Weidenfeld and Nicolson, 1964.

_____. *Nine Norse Studies*. London: Viking Society for Northern Research, 1972.

DID ANGLO-SAXON AUDIENCES HAVE
A SKALDIC TOOTH?

ROBERTA FRANK
University of Toronto

IT IS GENERALLY acknowledged that the Norse skalds had no discernible impact on Old English poetic style. A. H. Smith's conclusion of 1936 still holds: "We cannot point to any instances of skaldic influence. . .in English literature of the period."[1] By all rights my subject can be disposed of as briskly as that guidebook chapter, "Concerning Snakes in Iceland," that so intrigued Samuel Johnson; the chapter consists of one sentence, "There are no snakes of any kind in the whole island."[2]

One difference is that there were Scandinavians in England, so numerous and so influential that some historians of English prefer to speak of "an Anglo-Danish language rather than of English with high absorption of Scandinavian elements" (Strang 340). For most of the Anglo-Saxon period, the Danes and the English seem not to have formed discrete, mutually hostile communities. When the English-Scandinavians became literate it was in English; the coinage, inscriptions, sculpture, even poetry of the first Scandinavian settlers show them striving to be more Christian and English than the English.[3] And the compliment was returned, sometimes in unexpected ways.

Alcuin, in a letter written shortly after the viking attack on Lindisfarne in 793, rebuked his countrymen not only for singing of Ingeld but also for imitating the hairdos of the Northmen: "Consider the dress, the way of wearing the hair, the luxurious habits of the princes and people. Look at your hairstyle, how you have wished to resemble the pagans in your beards and hair. Are you not terrified of those whose hairstyle you wanted to have?"[4] Two hundred years later, in Ethelred's reign, Ælfric is still regretting this English weakness for Danish cuts: "I tell you also, brother Edward, since you have asked, that you (pl.) do wrong in forsaking the English customs that your fathers held, and in loving the customs of heathen men who begrudge you life, and you make it clear by these evil practices that you despise your people and your ancestors, since in insult to them you dress in Danish manner with bared necks and blinded eyes" (Pope 1:56).

English fashions in nonpersonal ornamentation, too, can be seen absorbing more and more Norse elements as time goes on. Around 900, new motifs, apparently reflecting contemporary Scandinavian design, start appearing on the stone crosses and slabs of Northern England, initiating a minor renaissance in Anglo-Saxon sculpture. In the early eleventh century, the period in which most of our poetic manuscripts were produced, there was a second influx of Scandinavian taste, visible, for example, in the animal head terminals of Noah's ark in the *Old English Hexateuch* (London, British Library MS Claudius B iv), and somewhat less clearly in a sketch for binding and clasps in the Cædmon Manuscript of Old English poetry (Oxford, Bodleian Library MS Junius 11; see Fuglesang 72–75). As on the stone carvings, the "viking" element in these drawings tends to be an isolated detail, an ornament in a design that is basically non-Scandinavian.

Locating comparable northern decoration in Old English poetry is far more difficult. Our science is weak: we cannot confidently distinguish ninth- and tenth-century compositions from earlier pieces, let alone Scandinavian imagery from native English or common Germanic literary motifs. There are only four certain examples of pre-viking English verse, all short and for various reasons unlikely to be representative of what once existed (Stanley 1974). Old Norse skaldic verse, sometimes datable and attributable to named authors, does not start until the second half of the ninth century and may itself have evolved in an insular context. My attempt to demonstrate that some Anglo-Saxon audiences were not immune to Norse taste has as its springboard the fact that certain lines of Old English verse are extraordinarily responsive to a "skaldic" reading. Indeed, there is one work, preserved in the Cædmon Manuscript, that seems to demand for its comprehension an audience trained in the special language of the skalds.

I

The Old English *Exodus* is a difficult, allusive poem, described by Levin Schücking in 1915 as the product of a school from which nothing else has survived.[5] The poet's language is at times startlingly different from that of his countrymen. At these moments his diction seems to be based on a system of conventions not unlike that underlying the kennings of the skalds. By 900, the Norse poets had constructed a separate syntax or language of metaphorical expression that usually depended for its decoding as much on previous knowledge and training as on a feeling for, or observation of, nature. In the earliest skaldic poem that has come down to us—Bragi's *Ragnarsdrápa*—the poet calls a painted shield first "blade of the footsoles of Þrúðr's thief" (a mythological allusion to a not-too-bright giant who, fearful of an underground attack, stood on his shield) and then, in rapid succession, "wheel" (of the valkyrie), "leaf" (of the trees of the sea), "bottom-land" (of the shield-boss), and—in the refrain—"moon" (of the sea king's chariot).[6] Each of these "metaphors" is a traditional name for "shield" in the special language of the skalds (Meissner 166–71). Their cumulative weight ensures that the painted shield, seen from a variety of incongruous perspectives, is never far from the listener's mind. The *Exodus* poet does something rather similar in one section of his narrative, apparently unconcerned about the possibility of losing his audience.

The passage in question has caused modern editors and commentators much grief. The poet is describing the pillar of cloud with which God shields the Israelites from the desert sun:

>   Þær halig God
> wið færbryne   folc gescylde,
> bælce oferbrædde   byrnendne heofon,
> halgan nette   hatwendne lyft.
> 75   Hæfde wederwolcen   widum fæðmum
> eorðan ond uprodor   efne gedæled,
> lædde leodwerod,   ligfyr adranc,
> hate heofontorht.   Hæleð wafedon,
> drihta gedrymost.   Dægsceldes hleo
> 80   wand ofer wolcnum.   Hæfde witig God
> sunnan siðfæt   segle ofertolden,
> swa þa mæstrapas   men ne cuðon
> ne ða seglrode   geseon meahton
> eorðbuende   ealle cræfte,
> 85   hu afæstnod wæs   feldhusa mæst. . .
>   [*Exodus* 71–85].

(There holy God shielded the people against the terrible fire; he covered over the burning heaven with a *board*, the scorching sky with a holy *net*. The *stormcloud* had with wide embraces evenly divided earth and heaven; it led the people; the flaming fire, skybright with heat, was quenched. Men marvelled, most joyful of troops. The protection of the *brightness-shield* moved across the sky. Wise God had tented over the course of the sun with a *sail*, so that men, earthdwellers, knew not those mast-ropes, could not by any cunning see that sailyard, how the greatest of *tents* was fastened. . . [my emphases].)

In the space of twelve lines, there are six different metaphors for the same object. In line 73 the pillar of cloud is called a *bælc* 'wooden board'; in line 74, *nett* 'net'; in line 75, *wederwolcen* 'stormcloud'; it is a *dægsceld* 'sun-shield, cloud' again in line 79; in line 81 the pillar becomes a *segl* 'sail'; in line 85, a *feldhus* 'tent'. Even Brodeur, an appreciative and sensitive reader, lost patience with the *Exodus* poet here:

What justification is there for denominating the pillar of cloud a "holy net" or a "sail"? It may well be called *lyfthelm*, "airy protective covering" [line 60] or a "canopy" [his reading of *bælc*]; "tent" (*feldhus*) is a little far-fetched. But "net," with its connotation of reticulation, is a distinctly bad comparison. . . . To me this figure of the sail, with its invisible mast, cables, and spars, seems grotesque [1968, 111].

Taste decides which passages in any work should be celebrated and which hanged by the neck until dead; modern readers faced with this gallimaufry tend to lean towards an execution. But if the audience of *Exodus* had a skaldic tooth, these fifteen lines would have given them something to bite into. For the three images that seemed most jarring to Brodeur—the tent, net, and sail—are, like board and cloud, traditional names or base words for "shield" in the special language of the skalds:[7]

	Some skaldic shield-kennings:
bælc 'board' (73)	vígbǫlkr, Viðris bǫlkr
nett 'net' (74)	oddnet, hjǫrnet, geirnet
wolcen 'cloud' (75)	rógský, Þundar ský, oddský
segl 'sail' (81)	rógsegl, Hlakkar segl, naglfara segl
feldhus 'tent' (85)	vígtjald, gunntjald, Yggjar tjald.

One skaldic primer tells the aspiring poet that "a shield can be named by any word for sun and moon, sky and cloud; it can also be called a wall or enclosure, a board (*bǫlkr*) and screen, a door and sill, a plank and lattice-work, shutter and sail, tent and wall-hanging, and it can always be defined by battle, Odin, or sea kings" (Jónsson 1931, 255). To an audience familiar with the common shield-kenning type represented above by *Viðris bǫlkr* 'Odin's board', *Þundar ský* 'Odin's cloud', and *Yggjar tjald* 'Odin's tent', the Old English poet's replacement of Odin with God (lines 71, 80) would have been pointed and unmistakable. The pillar of cloud, envisaged as a divine shield, supplants its counterpart in Norse mythology, the sun-god's shield called Svǫl 'the cooling' that kept the world from bursting into flame (Neckel 65; Jónsson 1912, 665).

In lines 71–85, then, the *Exodus* poet mentally converts the pillar of cloud into a shield (its stated function) and calls up, one by one, five common skaldic names or synonyms for shield, probing the connotations of each. The board and lattice-work contraptions (*bælc* and *nett*) are put into place to screen heaven, preventing the escape of hot coals; a moisture-laden cloud (*wederwolcen*) arrives to quench the fire; mention of a sail launches some richly allusive nautical imagery, uncovering a mast, crossbar, and rigging; the tent metaphor (*feldhus*), hiding all in its folds, serves as a final image of homecoming. Each image is linked to the others through learned, not visual, association. And through these metaphors, the Israelites shielded by God on the journey to the Red Sea become a figure of the Christian embraced by the Ship of the Church (Earl 1970,

Lucas 1970).

Little is knowable and less is certain in the study of Old English style. *Exodus* was probably composed somewhere in England, sometime between 700 and 1000. If the poem is taken to be very early, its skaldic symptoms will be attributed to a common fifth- and sixth-century North Sea poetic idiom or, if medium early, to a late eighth- and early ninth-century oral style elaborated in the new viking colonies of Ireland and Britain. (This method, sometimes called triangulation and derived from a linguistic model, when applied to literary questions usually ends up, as here, explaining two unknowns by an unknowable.) But if the poem is merely early (and early in Old English terms means not later than 950), there is a third possibility, that the "viking" motifs and details of *Exodus* reflect a late ninth- or early tenth-century renovation of Cædmonian poetry, Scandinavian decoration embellishing, as on the stone crosses, a distinctively English religious art. I am partial to this last scenario, the impossibility of which cannot be conclusively proved.

II

Exodus has the highest proportion of different compounds per line of any of the longer Old English poems; *Beowulf* is next (Carr 414). Nevertheless, as Schücking also observed in 1915, the two poems were intended for very different audiences (16). Not only is a knowledge of kenning types not needed by anyone listening to *Beowulf*, but it can even be counterproductive. There is little advantage, for example, in being able to recognize that *net* is a base word in skaldic kennings for shield when Beowulf appears fully encased in a *herenet* 'battle-net' (1553) and *breostnet* 'breast-net' (1548):[8] *net*-compounds in *Beowulf* designate chain-mail, not shields (Mohr 31). The poet's vivid kenning *hildegicel* 'battle-icicle' (1606) would in the skalds' metalanguage signify 'sword' (ON *hildar jǫkull, bǫðvar jǫkull*); but in *Beowulf* it is used descriptively, to portray how the hero's sword literally melted in the monster's blood. Brodeur commended the poet for his naturalness here: the image is "not concealed and strained as in the skaldic kenning" (1959, 22). Indeed, to make sure that his picture of a sword wasting away in battle-icicles is not ignored or misunderstood, the poet quickly adds: "It all melted, just like ice" (1608). The compounds *beaduleoma* and *hildeleoma* 'battle-light', kennings for sword in Old Norse, refer in lines 1523 and 2583 of *Beowulf* to sword flashes and dragon flame; this literal meaning—'battle-light'—is so alive in the poem that, when the poet in line 1143 uses *hildeleoma* as a sword-kenning, he immediately varies it with the explanatory gloss: "best of swords."[9] The *Beowulf* poet's insistent clarifications effectively underline the foreignness of his "harder" compounds, the pastness of his past. His echoes of skaldic diction seem to be heard at a great distance, from outside the tradition, and recorded to supply a touch of Scandinavian color, to capture the flavor of the sixth-century Danish society described.

In the *Beowulf* poet's reconstruction of his northern society, special prominence is given to strong drink, with the terms for ale, mead, wine, and liqueur used synonymously as interchangeable lexical units. Such substitutions are common in skaldic verse in which, in the kenning types "drink of the raven" for blood or "drink of Odin" for poetry, any word for liquid—from ale to sea—will do. In *Beowulf*, Heorot is both a meadhall and a winehall; its inhabitants grow mellow on mead-benches and ale-benches. One man's *ealuscerwen* 'ale-pouring' (*Beowulf* 769) is another man's *meoduscerwen* 'mead-pouring' (*Andreas* 1526). Wealhtheow, like an absent-minded hostess, is seen handing out meadcups at the royal beer-party, resembling in her distraction the highly domesticated valkyries of the skaldic *Eiríksmál* who serve wine but wash beer-mugs. (Incidentally, this beer [OE *beor*, ON *bjórr*] was not a malt-based drink, but a sweet fruit liqueur [Fell 1975].) The interchangeability in *Beowulf* of words for strong drink can be, and has been, shrugged off as simple variation, but it is curious that the poet does not treat his terms for warriors or weapons in so cavalier a fashion; most fit their contexts like a glove (Brady 1979 and 1983). The *Heliand* poet, even at his most Germanic, does not treat incompatible items as synonyms, mixing different sword-types or drinks. In what is perhaps his purplest passage, containing four expressions for sword, the Old Saxon author uses the specifying *bil* and *mece*, alongside the generic *sweord* and *heoru*, to indicate that Peter is brandishing a long two-edged hewing sword, not the shorter blade (*seax, secg, brand*) designed for thrusting:

> ...ac hie is *bill* atoh,
> *sverd* be sidu,   sluog im tegegnes
> an thena furiston fiond   folmo craftu,
> that thuo Malchus uuarth   *makies* eggion
> an thia suithrun half   *suerdu* gimalod;
> thiu hlust uuarth im farhauuan: hie uuarth an that hobid uund,
> that im *heru*drorag   hlier endi ora
> benuundun brast   [4872–79; my emphases].[10]

> (. . .but he drew his sword,
> the sword by his side,   he thrust out
> at the enemy leader   with the power of his hand,
> so that Malchus was   by the edges of the sword
> on his right side   marked by the sword.
> His hearing was hewn: he was wounded in the head,
> so that sword-bloody   his cheek and ear
> burst in wounds.)

The *Heliand* poet's two drinking parties (1994–2076, 2733–42) are equally conservative, allowing only *win* and *lið*, wine and alcoholic fruit drink, to be imbibed, beverages as interchangeable on the dinner table as in verse. But, although you will never catch Anglo-Saxons substituting mead, fruit liqueur, or wine for ale anywhere but in poetry, such variations are normal procedure in much of their verse and in the verse of the skalds.

Anglo-Saxon authors seem to have had two distinct lexicons at their disposal, that of poetry and that of prose. The two discourses are separated from each other by a semantic shift as far-reaching as any sound change. Sometimes the Old Norse cognate of an English word seems to help in establishing the latter's meaning in *Beowulf*. The notorious *lofgeornost*, for example, which in Old English prose has the sense 'too eager for praise', in Old Norse verse as in *Beowulf* appears to mean 'most eager for praise', while *dollic*, 'foolish' in Old English homiletic contexts, in Old Norse verse as in *Beowulf* seems to mean 'bold, ready to risk'.[11] The language of poetry tends to be general and metaphorical, without reference to spatial or visual shape (or in the case of mead and ale, taste); that of prose is particularistic and allusive, treating local variations in size, altitude, dampness, hue, and material as distinct entities (in prose, a honey-derived drink is not the same as a malt-based liquor). The prose word also tends to be more abstract. Thus *sund* in Old English poetry signifies 'sea', but in prose it stands for the abstract act or power of 'swimming', a mental construct separate from the physical world of nature.[12] In skaldic and eddic verse of the tenth, eleventh, and early twelfth century, *sund* means 'sea, sound', as it still does in modern Swedish, Danish, and Norwegian. The one glaring exception to the rule that *sund* in poetry means 'sea' is *Beowulf*, whose editors and translators are unanimous in giving a prose sense to certain occurrences of the term.[13] The two instances I want to look at are prominent in Unferth's version of Beowulf's adventure with Breca: "ymb sund flite" ("you competed at swimming" 507) and "he þe æt sunde oferflat" ("he defeated you at swimming" 517). Midway between these verses, Unferth refers to the "sea" on which Beowulf and Breca "rowed" ("on sund reon" 512), a half line repeated by Beowulf in his reply to Unferth (539). *Sund*, whether 'sea' or 'swimming', is not a common word in Old English. It occurs uncompounded only six times in prose and twenty-six times in verse, a frequency of less than once every thousand lines of poetry. (*Exodus*, for example, despite its abundance of waters, does not have a single *sund*.) Unferth, in his opening twelve lines, uses the term three times, a concentration without parallel in the corpus.

The notion that Beowulf and Breca were contenders in a swimming match got started early. Although Thorkelin retained a manuscript reading that allowed for a vessel in the neighborhood of his hero, Grundtvig's translation of *Beowulf* kept the two boys in the water for a week, "swimming like two fish, and soon like dead herring" (48), a view that understandably won the day.[14] Not until the 1960s and 1970s was the textual evidence for Beowulf's long-distance swimming reexamined and found wanting; the two studies concerned solely with the Unferth episode concluded that the thyle's twin references to a swimming match should be translated as "you competed at rowing" and "he defeated you at rowing," respectively (Wentersdorf, Earl 1979). Unferth would have been delighted at the controversy he initiated, especially if he had deliberately created a "gap" of indeterminacy by employing *sund* in both its poetic and prose senses simultaneously, keeping a handle on the truth while insinuating something quite different.

Swimming and rowing, floating and sailing, even flying and jogging are such closely related notions, sharing the same "ground," that conceptual interchanges between them are easy to grasp: boats move on limbs and swim; swimmers fling their oars and skim the waves. There is universal agreement that one of these two metaphoric equations is present in Unferth's opening lines, but which of the two and where are disputed. The traditional view takes Unferth's single reference to rowing in line 512 metaphorically ('swim'), and the five ornate half lines that follow literally, as a description of arms at swim. But it is at least as likely that these five half lines contain the figurative meaning 'rowing', as do the comparable expressions "hreran mid handum" ("stirring [the sea] with hands," *Wanderer* 4) and "mere hrerendum mundum" ("with hands stirring the sea," *Andreas* 491); the humble prose word 'to row', which never has the sense 'to swim' outside *Beowulf*, is more likely to be a clarifying element, resolving the ambiguity initiated five lines earlier by "ymb sund flite" ("contended around the sea"):

> ... þa git on sund reon;
> þær git eagorstream   earmum þehton,
> mæton merestræta,   mundum brugdon,
> glidon ofer garsecg. . .   [512–15].

> (. . .when you two rowed to sea;
> there the two of you covered   the flowing tide with arms,
> spanned the sea-paths,   flung hands,
> glided over the ocean. . . .)

Like his initial and final *sund* (507, 517), the four verbs used by Unferth to depict the action—*þehton, mæton, brugdon, glidon*—are doublevalenced terms appropriate to swimming as well as rowing. Swimmers conceivably "glide" in Old English; ships definitely do. Arms without oars can "thatch" the sea almost as well as arms with them. And the expression *mundum brugdon*, which has the boys hauling themselves along with their hands, may allude to swimming (at least a dog-paddle) but can also, and perhaps more easily, refer to the wielding of oars, as in *arum bregdað* 'they ply oars' (*Gifts of Men*, 57). The poet could have distinguished between swimming and rowing in these lines simply by substituting feet (*fotum brugdon* 'kicked') or oars (*arum brugdon* 'rowed') for hands; but he didn't care to. The progression in Unferth's speech from rowing to covering with arms, spanning, flinging hands, and gliding is a movement from specificity to ambiguity, from the real to the disguised.

Hamlet—in Saxo and in Shakespeare—always speaks the truth, but in such a way that his answers, which depend on a literal interpretation of metaphor or familiar poetic imagery, are misconstrued by his hearers. The Old Norse skald was skilled in this kind of duplicity, turning blame into praise, a monk's tonsure into the cutting down of trees, a sailing ship into a lumbering bear. On a much more elementary level, Unferth seems to be playing the same skaldic game of disguises, riddling in such a way as to make his meaning clear to the initiated and misleading to the naive. Beowulf shows what a consummate solver he is by "reading" Unferth's verses correctly and by inserting as answer in his reply the thyle's one unambiguous reference to rowing: *on sund reon* (512, 539), a recognizable half-line formula in Old Norse verse (*á vág róa,   á sió róa* ['to row to sea']), in which *sund* has to mean 'sea'. And when Beowulf adds that he and Breca rowed to sea with, not oars, but "bare swords firm in hand" (539), there is just a chance that he may be repaying Unferth in skaldic coin, for in the inverse world of the kenning "oars of wounds" and "oars of battle" cleave skulls as well as waves (Meissner 153).

That the Unferth episode is a set piece, related in an immediate and exact way to the Old Norse flyting, has been demonstrated by Carol Clover. The disjunctions, silent riddles, and obliqueness characteristic of the genre would have been challengingly meaningful to audiences raised on such fare, but outsiders—even Saxo, in his Latin rendition of Eric the Eloquent's verbal gymnastics—have always found them impenetrable. Not expecting this kind of subtlety or wit in a traditional poem like *Beowulf*, we, too, miss the cue: we take Unferth's *ymb sund* and *æt sunde* in a prose sense, convert the literal 'rowed' to 'swam', and attribute the consequent "strained use of words" to the poet's unthinking dependence on a preexisting heroic lay (Campbell 284). Obfuscation is taken as elucidation; what was straight is made crooked; and we conclude finally that the poet did not know what he was doing. But darkness was not the *Beowulf* poet's way. Unferth's sinuous, ornate diction, his arrogant bow-wow, stands rhetorically apart from its matrix, a Scandinavian ornament set in an English poem.

III

Unferth's flyting with Beowulf, as Clover has shown, exhibits a typical sequence of Claim, Defense, and Counterclaim (452). The present paper has, unintentionally, somewhat the same structure. I began by citing passages from *Exodus* and *Beowulf* that seemed to me to cast doubt on the assertion that the Norse skalds had no influence on Old English poetic style. If my final remarks now take the form of a counterclaim, it is because—like Beowulf—I want to provoke, to challenge the received version of an oft-told story. In a recent and excellent article on *Exodus*, Thomas Hill concludes that "the poet does not simply draw upon traditional Germanic diction, he revels in it and in several instances at least uses traditional images in a way which reflects a genuinely sophisticated command of German poetic idiom" (64). Hill gives as an example of such Germanic diction the phrase *ecg grymetode* 'the sword roared' (*Exodus* 408), in which a verb normally used of lions is applied to a drawn blade. The half line occurs nowhere else in Old English; it is unknown in Frisian, Old Saxon, Old Low Franconian, Old High German, and Gothic; but there are exact parallels in the verse of the skalds (*Lexicon Poeticum*, s.v. *grenja* 'to roar'). The evidence does not suggest to me that what is distinctive in the diction of *Exodus* derives from the inherited poetry of continental Germania. To conclude that it does is to treat the literatures of the various German-speaking lands between 400 and 1000 as if they were one and to regard medieval Scandinavia as a kind of *Germania germanicissima*, preserving untarnished an antiquity that others rather carelessly lost.[15]

Over the years the scholarship of Old English literature has tended to accept both these propositions as self-evident. It is traditional, for example, to see the wolf, raven, and eagle that together dine off the slain in eight Old English poems and hundreds of skaldic stanzas as relics of a distant Germanic past.[16] In Jacob Grimm's words, "All this. . .breathes the oldest poetry of our antiquity. Let us remember that these three animals were considered noble, brave, a portent of good luck, sacred to the highest god" (xxvii, trans. Stanley 1975, 16). Maybe so, but he could have mentioned that these three camp-followers never show their faces in continental Germanic literature. Birds and beasts devouring the fallen are, to be sure, not unknown outside the North Sea littoral. Psalm 79.2 laments: "They have thrown out the dead bodies of thy servants to feed the birds of the air; they have made thy loyal servants carrion for wild beasts." In ninth-century Europe, Florus of Lyons reports "both wild beasts and birds" at the battle of Fontenoy; Angelbert, an eyewitness to the same battle, comments on its vultures, crows, and wolves; Radbod is impressed by the fastidiousness of a wolf and raven that preferred their carrion fresh.[17] Yet none of these Carolingian notices seems related in any direct or detailed way to the companionable triads of Old English and Old Norse poetry.

Why have we refused to see the beasts of battle in Old English poetry as possible northern decoration, beloved ornamental motifs, like those animal-head terminals on Noah's ship? The *Beowulf* passage containing the three boon companions takes the form of a reported conversation:

> . . .ac se wonna hrefn
> fus ofer fægum   fela reordian,

earne secgan,   hu him æt æte speow,
þenden he wið wulf   wæl reafode
[3024–27].

(. . .but the black raven
eager over doomed men   [will] speak much,
say to the eagle   how he fared at the feast
when he strove with the wolf   to strip the corpses.)

The messenger's vision of a raven speaking to his dinner partner about a gourmet treat has skaldic parallels: a particularly garrulous raven, called *arnar eiðbróðir* 'sworn brother of the eagle', does much of the talking in Þorbjǫrn Hornklofi's *Haraldskvæði* (circa 900); in the eddic *Helgakviða Hundingsbana I*, one raven tells another that they'll soon rejoice with the wolf; while in *Brot af Sigurðarkviðu* the speech of raven and eagle warns a hero of trouble ahead. The *Beowulf* poet's feat of compression— three interlaced beasts in seven half lines—is also reminiscent of skaldic technique. The poet Grani managed to fit the raven, eagle, and wolf into a single eight-line stanza (Jónsson 1912, 357). Þórmóðr Trefilsson achieved somewhat the same result in four lines (of only five syllables each) by placing one of the three beasts in a warrior kenning: "The feeder of the raven [here called "swan of blood"] sated the eagle on the food of the wolf" (Jónsson 1912, 196).

The beasts-of-battle passage in *Exodus* contains four *hapax legomena*, each of which seems to allude to a familiar skaldic motif:

Hreopon herefugolas   hilde grædige,
deawigfeðere   ofer *drihtneum*,
wonn *wælceasega*.   Wulfas sungon
atol æfenleoð   ætes on wenan,
carleasan deor,   *cwyldrof* beodan
on laðra last   leodmægnes f[y]l.
Hreopon *mearcweardas*   middum nihtum. . .
[162–68; my emphases].

(The carrion birds cried out   greedy for battle,
dewy-feathered   over warrior-corpses,
the dark chooser of the slain.   Wolves sang
a terrible evening song   in expectation of feasting,
beasts unpitying,   evening-bold they announced
behind the foe   the slaughter of the people's army.
Borderland-guardians cried out   in the middle of the night. . . .)

The *Exodus* poet's *wælceasega*, apparently made in imitation of Old English *wælcyrige*, Old Norse *valkyrja*, *valkjósandi* 'chooser of the slain', recalls both the raven's privileges on the battlefield and the valkyries of Norse mythology who hover over the fighting warriors and, in the words of one skald, have their "choice of the slain." The Old English poet here reduces the Norse battlefield goddesses to a swarm of greedy, noisy birds, a secularization or euhemerization of Norse story. The second compound, the mysterious *dryhtneas*, recalls the frequent use in skaldic raven kennings of the definer *nár* 'corpse', the Old Norse cognate of the much rarer Old English *ne* (e.g., *ná-gagl* 'corpse-crow', *ná-haukr* 'corpse-hawk', *ná-skari* 'corpse-bird', *nás gammr* 'vulture of the slain', *nás nagr* 'bird of the slain'). *Cwyldrof*, the third compound, is a reminder that wolves in skaldic kennings tend to be characterized not as corpse-pickers but as the mounts of giantesses, trollwives, or witches, steeds of the *kveldriða* 'one who rides in the evening'; the *Exodus* poet's *cwyld*, apparently cognate with ON *kveld*, places the wolf in this ominous twilight world. The final term, *mearcweardas* 'borderland-guardians', probably designates the same wolves that, a few lines later, merge with the demonic Egyptians, those "sword-wolves" massed in their "borderland-troop." Scops and skalds traditionally locate their wolves in woods (cf. OE *wulf on wealde*), which happens to be the sense of Old Norse *mǫrk*, the cognate of *mearc*. Just as the Old Norse reflexes of *lofgeornost* and *dollic* are guides to their meaning in *Beowulf*, so here *mǫrk* reminds us that *mearc* in poetry has a concrete, generalized meaning ('uninhabited territory') that encompasses 'woods'. Through these four compounds, the screaming and yelping beasts of *Exodus* are given what, to my ears at least, sounds like a northern accent, as if the poet wanted to supply his audience's craving for what they had always had, to indulge their skaldic tooth.

In discussions of the beasts of battle, Anglo-Saxonists have tended to treat as "German" an image of dissolution that has a much wider currency (as in the Psalms) and have called "Teutonic" a decorative triad whose mutual assistance pact has a much narrower currency, limited as it is to Old Norse verse and eight Old English poems, at least two of which (*Maldon* and *Brunanburh*) are clearly post-viking. Tracing the origins of this prejudice, this Germanic bias, takes us back to the very beginnings of Anglo-Saxon scholarship. William Camden (1551–1623), an admirer of contemporary German humanism and a man for whom Tacitus was a favorite author, was the first English scholar to concern himself with the national origins of the Anglo-Saxons. In *Remains Concerning Britain,* published in 1605, about the time Shakespeare was writing *Lear* and *Macbeth,* he stressed Germanic descent: "This English tongue is extracted, as the nation, from the Germans, the most glorious of all now extant in Europe. . ." (23). In the same year, Richard Verstegen's *Restitution of Decayed Intelligence* appeared, a panegyric to the Germanic heritage of the English. The Scandinavian connection was, in his view, irrelevant. The Danish and Norman settlers, he explained, were so few that they did not alter the original Saxon purity; and anyway, he added, they "were once one same people with the Germans, as were also the Saxons" (187). In his *Thesaurus* of 1705, George Hickes, the first to describe Old English poetry, divided its production into three periods: British (or Pure) Saxon, Dano-Saxon, and Norman (or Semi-Saxon). Pure Saxon is *Cædmon's Hymn*; the remaining verse is in Dano-Saxon, which he blamed on the Danes, "a rude and an illiterate People in all Respects, and for the most part Pirates, [who] corrupted the Anglo-Saxon language."[18] Over the next hundred years, this Dano-Saxon poetry was gradually pushed back into the earlier, Pure Saxon phase, where its Germanic qualities could shine in unadulterated splendor.

Modern Anglo-Saxon scholarship, as Eric Stanley has vividly demonstrated, was born of the Romantic movement, at a time when Germany was the center of the world of Germanic philology. From the German perspective, Old English poetry was a segment of German literature that had been temporarily alienated. Anglo-Saxon, wrote Heinrich Leo in 1838, "was then, and has remained ever since, a German dialect in the strictest sense of the word" (10–11, cited by Stanley 1975, 5). Whatever in the verse was not obviously Mediterranean in inspiration was Germanic or Teutonic. Sir Francis Palgrave, stressing in 1832 the remote antiquity of the Cædmonian poems, assured his readers that they belonged "not only to Englishmen, but to every branch of the great Teutonic family."[19] The ninth- and tenth-century viking colonization of Northern and Eastern England, Man, Ireland, and Scotland was too late, even too Christian, to be included in that family tree.

Linguists and art historians see things somewhat differently today. They tell us we are mistaken if we think of Anglo-Saxon England as essentially an English population with a few Danish accretions. "When the outcome of the fusion of the two languages was written," observed Barbara Strang, "it was written in an extension of the English tradition, and so appears as a variety of English. Culturally it was; a modern reader must beware of reading national meaning into such a claim" (383). The evidence amassed by art historians points to an integration of Scandinavian motifs with English traditions, a reciprocity and blending, not a stifling of one by the other. If Old English poetry alone of the arts did not "catch" Scandinavian taste, its immunity needs explaining.

In emphasizing similarities between *Beowulf* and *Exodus* and their skaldic neighbors, I have tried to indicate some ways in which we can profit from comparative studies of this kind. Sometimes light is shed on the meaning of individual words or on the interpretation of a puzzling passage; sometimes the local effects that a poet sought with his figures become a little clearer. And sometimes we get glimpses, far off, of a differently shaped, differently motivated, differently worded history of Old English poetry, waiting impatiently to be written.

---

[1] Smith 223. See, too, Stanley 1985, 265: "Nevertheless I prefer Rieger's feeble interpretation to Malone's imaginative Skaldicism; the latter requires knowledge to which we have access, but which the Anglo-Saxons are not likely to have had."

² Hill and Powell 3:279. The guidebook referred to was Niels Horrebow, *Tilforladelige efterretninger om Island* (Copenhagen, 1752) ch. 72; an English translation appeared in 1758.

³ See, for example, Lang; Morris; Bailey; Wilson; Hofmann 1955; and Okasha, 41, 47, 88, 114–17, 126–27, 131.

⁴ "Considerate habitum, tonsuram, et mores principum et populi luxuriosos. Ecce tonsura, quam in barbis et in capillis paganis adsimilari voluistis. Nonne illorum terror inminet quorum tonsuram habere voluistis?" See Dümmler 43; Chase 55; Whitelock 843.

⁵ Schücking 16. Two editions of *Exodus* have recently appeared, Lucas 1977 and Turville-Petre 1981. This paper also makes use of notes and commentary in Irving 1953 and 1972.

⁶ All skaldic quotations in this paper are from Jónsson 1912.

⁷ First noted by Hofmann 1957, 24. Irving, rejecting skaldic influence, argued that the poet's metaphors are not "really kennings at all, as Hofmann concedes when he refers to them as 'Halbkenningar'" (1959, 7). Lucas concurs that "there is no evidence of Old Norse influence" (1977, 71).

⁸ References to *Beowulf* are from Fr. Klaeber, ed., *Beowulf and the Fight at Finnsburg*, 3rd ed. (Boston: Heath, 1950).

⁹ On clarifying variation in *Beowulf* (and *hildeleoma* in particular) see Robinson 130–32.

¹⁰ Text from London, British Library MS Cotton Caligula A.vii, in Eduard Sievers, ed. *Heliand*, Germanistische Handbibliothek 4 (Halle, 1878); my translation.

¹¹ Old English lexicographical information in this paper comes from *A Microfiche Concordance to Old English*, ed. Antonette diPaolo Healey and Richard L. Venezky (Toronto: Pontifical Institute of Mediaeval Studies, 1980); Old Norse, from Finnur Jónsson, *Lexicon poeticum antiquae linguae septentrionalis. . .af Sveinbjörn Egilsson*, 2nd ed. (Copenhagen: Møller, 1931); Johan Fritzner, *Ordbog over det gamle norske Sprog*, vols. 1–3 (Oslo, 1883–96), and vol. 4 (*Supplement* by Finn Hødnebø, Oslo: Universitetsforlaget, 1972); and Richard Cleasby and Gudbrand Vigfusson, *An Icelandic-English Dictionary*, 2nd ed. with supplement by Sir William A. Craigie (Oxford: Clarendon, 1957).

¹² There are only two exceptions to this rule outside *Beowulf*. The sense 'swimming' is found in poetry in *Solomon and Saturn*, a late, apparently West Saxon composition with a high incidence of prosaic words. And in Ælfric's homily on Cuthbert, which is a rhythmical composition, *sund* means 'sea'. *Sund* is often said to be a common word for 'swimming' in Old Norse, but there is no certain evidence for this usage before the late twelfth century, and then chiefly in prose.

¹³ *Sund* is glossed 'swimming' in *Beowulf* 507, 517, 1436, and 1618. See, also, Frank 158–72.

¹⁴ In Danish, "dead as a herring" means dead as a doornail.

¹⁵ Von See points out that this exaltation of Scandinavia as preserver of the heritage of the continental Germanic tribes is a phenomenon of nineteenth-century German scholarship (34–37).

¹⁶ I count as beasts-of-battle passages *Brunanburh* 60–65; *Beowulf* 3024–27; *Elene* 27–30, 110–16; *Exodus* 161–69; *Finnsburh* 5–7, 34–35; *Genesis A* 1183–85, 2157–61; *Judith* 204–12, 292–96; and *Maldon* 106–07. I exclude *Wanderer* 81–83 and *Fates* 10–14, 33–42, in which a bird or wolf—outside the context of battle—simply disposes of a corpse. Warriors, by killing or being killed, provide food for raven, eagle, and wolf in some early Welsh battle poetry. See, for example, Kenneth H. Jackson, *The Gododdin: The Oldest Scottish Poem* (Edinburgh: University of Edinburgh Press, 1969) 41.

¹⁷ Godman 49–50, 264 (no. 39: 14), 270 (no. 40: 100). For classical and (additional) Christian Latin precedents see Brown 35–37.

¹⁸ William Wotton, *Hickesii Thesauri Grammatico-Critici Conspectus Brevis* (London, 1708), trans. by Maurice Shelton as *Wotton's Short View of George Hickes's Grammatico-Critical and Archaeological Treasures of the Ancient Northern Languages* (London, 1735) 11; cited by Calder 4.

¹⁹ Francis Palgrave, *Archaeologia* 24 (1832): 343, cited by Stanley 1975, 6.

WORKS CITED

Bailey, Richard. *Viking Age Sculpture in Northern England*. London: Collins, 1980.

Brady, Caroline. "'Warriors' in *Beowulf*: An Analysis of the Nominal Compounds and an Evaluation of the Poet's Use of Them." *Anglo-Saxon England* 11 (1983): 199–246.

——. "'Weapons' in *Beowulf*: An Analysis of the Nominal Compounds and an Evaluation of the Poet's Use of Them." *Anglo-Saxon England* 8 (1979): 79–141.

Brodeur, Arthur G. *The Art of Beowulf*. Berkeley: University of California Press, 1959.

——. "Three Anglo-Saxon Narrative Poems." *Nordica et Anglica: Studies in Honor of Stefan Einarsson*. Ed. Allan Orrick. The Hague: Mouton, 1968.

Brown, George Hardin. "An Iconographic Explanation of 'The Wanderer,' Lines 81b–82a." *Viator* 9 (1978): 31–38.

Calder, Daniel G. "The Study of Style in Old English Poetry: A Historical Introduction." *Old English Poetry: Essays on Style*. Ed. Daniel Calder. Berkeley: University of California Press, 1979. 1–65.

Camden, William. *Remains Concerning Britain*. Ed. R. D. Dunn. Toronto: University of Toronto Press, 1984.

Campbell, Alistair. "The Use in *Beowulf* of Earlier Heroic Verse." *England Before the Conquest: Studies in Primary Sources Presented to Dorothy Whitelock*. Ed. Peter Clemoes and Kathleen Hughes. Cambridge: Cambridge University Press, 1971. 283–92.

Carr, C. T. *Nominal Compounds in Germanic*. London: Oxford University Press, 1939.

Chase, Colin, ed. *Two Alcuin Letter-Books*. Toronto: Pontifical Institute of Mediaeval Studies, 1975.

Clover, Carol. "The Germanic Context of the Unferþ Episode." *Speculum* 55 (1980): 444–68.

Dümmler, Ernst L., ed. *Alcuini Epistolae*. Monumenta Germaniae Historica, Epistolae Karolini Aevi II. Berlin, 1895.

Earl, James W. "Beowulf's Rowing Match." *Neophilologus* 63 (1979): 285–90.

——. "Christian Tradition in the Old English *Exodus*." *Neuphilologische Mitteilungen* 71 (1970): 541–70.

Fell, Christine. "Old English *beor*." *Leeds Studies in English*. New series 8 (1975): 76–95.

Frank, Roberta. "*Mere* and *Sund*: Two Sea-Changes in *Beowulf*." *Modes of Interpretation in Old English Literature: Essays in Honour of Stanley B. Greenfield*. Ed. P. R. Brown, G. R. Crampton, and F. C. Robinson. Toronto: University of Toronto Press, 1986. 153–72.

Fuglesang, Signe Horn. *Some Aspects of the Ringerike Style: A Phase of Eleventh Century Scandinavian Art*. Odense: Odense University Press, 1980.

Godman, Peter. *Poetry of the Carolingian Renaissance*. London: Duckworth, 1985.

Grimm, Jacob, ed. *Andreas und Elene*. Cassel, 1840.

Grundtvig, N. F. S. *Bjowulfs drape: Et gothisk helte-digt fra forrige aar-tusinde af angelsaxisk paa danske riim*. Copenhagen, 1820.

Hill, George Birkbeck, ed. *Boswell's Life of Johnson*. Rev. L. F. Powell. 2nd ed. Oxford: Clarendon Press, 1964.

Hill, Thomas. "The *Virga* of Moses and the Old English *Exodus*." *Old English Literature in Context*. Ed. John D. Niles. Cambridge and Totowa, N.J.: D. S. Brewer, 1980. 57–65.

Hofmann, Dietrich. *Nordisch-englische Lehnbeziehungen der Wikingerzeit*. Bibliotheca Arnamagnæana 14. Copenhagen: E. Munksgaard, 1955.

——. "Untersuchungen zu den altenglischen Gedichten *Genesis* und *Exodus*." *Anglia* 75 (1957): 1–34.

Irving, Edward B. "New Notes on the Old English *Exodus*." *Anglia* 90 (1972): 289–324.

——, ed. *The Old English Exodus*. Yale Studies in English, 122. New Haven: Yale University Press, 1953.

——. "On the Dating of the Old English Poems *Genesis* and *Exodus*." *Anglia* 77 (1959): 1–11.

Jónsson, Finnur, ed. *Edda Snorra Sturlusonar*. Copenhagen: Gyldendalske Boghandel, 1931.

_____, ed. *Den norsk-islandske skjaldedigtning*. Vol. B., part 1. Copenhagen: Gyldendalske Boghandel, 1912.

Lang, James T. "Continuity and Innovation in Anglo-Scandinavian Sculpture." *Anglo-Saxon and Viking Age Sculpture and Its Context*. Ed. James T. Lang. British Archaeological Reports, British Series 49. Oxford: Bar, 1978. 145–72.

Leo, Heinrich. *Altsächsische und angelsächsische Sprachproben*. Halle, 1838.

Lucas, Peter J. "The Cloud in the Interpretation of the Old English *Exodus*." *English Studies* 51 (1970): 297–311.

_____, ed. *Exodus*. London: Methuen, 1977.

Meissner, Rudolf. *Die Kenningar der Skalden: Ein Beitrag zur skaldischen Poetik*. Rheinische Beiträge und Hülfsbücher zur germanischen Philologie und Volkskunde 1. Bonn: K. Schroeder, 1921.

Mohr, Wolfgang. *Kenningstudien: Beiträge zur Stilgeschichte der altgermanischen Dichtung*. Stuttgart: W. Kohlhammer, 1933.

Morris, C. D. "Pre-Conquest Sculpture of the Tees Valley." *Medieval Archaeology* 20 (1976): 140–46.

Neckel, Gustav, ed. *Edda*. I: *Text*. 5th ed. rev. Hans Kuhn. Heidelberg: C. Winter, 1983.

Okasha, Elisabeth. *Hand-List of Anglo-Saxon Non-Runic Inscriptions*. Cambridge: Cambridge University Press, 1971.

Pope, John C., ed. *Homilies of Ælfric: A Supplementary Collection*. 2 vols. Early English Text Society 259, 260. London: Oxford University Press, 1967–68.

Robinson, Fred C. "Two Aspects of Variation." *Old English Poetry: Essays on Style*. Ed. Daniel G. Calder. Berkeley: University of California Press, 1979. 127–46.

Schücking, Levin. *Untersuchungen zur Bedeutungslehre der angelsächsischen Dichtersprache*. Germanische Bibliothek 11. Heidelberg: C. Winter, 1915.

See, Klaus von. *Deutsche Germanen-Ideologie von Humanismus bis zum Gegenwart*. Frankfurt: Athenäum, 1970.

Smith, A. H. "The Early Literary Relations of England and Scandinavia." *Saga-Book of the Viking Society for Northern Research* 11 (1928–36): 215–32.

Stanley, E. G. "The Oldest English Poetry Now Extant." Poetica (Tokyo) 2 (1974): 1–24.

_____. *The Search for Anglo-Saxon Paganism*. Cambridge and Totowa, N. J.: D. S. Brewer, 1975. First published as articles in *Notes and Queries* 209 (1964): 204–09, 242–50, 282–87, 324–31, 455–63; and 210 (1965): 9–17, 203–07, 285–93, 322–27.

_____. "Unideal Principles of Editing Old English Verse." Sir Israel Gollancz Memorial Lecture 1984, British Academy Proceedings 70 (London 1985): 231–73.

Strang, Barbara M. H. *A History of English*. London: Methuen, 1970.

Thorkelin, G. J. *De Danorum rebus gestis secul. III et IV. Poëma Danicum dialecto Anglo-Saxonica*. Copenhagen, 1815.

Turville-Petre, Joan, ed. *The Old English Exodus: Text, Translation, and Commentary*. By J. R. R. Tolkien. Oxford: Clarendon Press, 1981. (Based on lectures delivered by Tolkien in the 1930s and 1940s)

Verstegen, Richard (Rowlands). *A Restitution of Decayed Intelligence: In Antiquities. Concerning the Most Noble and Renowned English Nation*. Antwerp, 1605; rpt. Amsterdam and Norwood, N. J.: W. J. Johnson, 1979.

Wentersdorf, Karl P. "Beowulf's Adventure with Breca." *Studies in Philology* 72 (1975): 140–66.

Whitelock, Dorothy, ed. *English Historical Documents: Volume 1, c. 500–1042*. 2nd ed. London: Eyre and Methuen, 1979.

Wilson, D. M. "The Scandinavians in England." *The Archaeology of Anglo-Saxon England*. Ed. David M. Wilson. New York: Methuen, 1977. 393–403.

SKALDIC TECHNIQUE IN *BRUNANBURH*

JOHN D. NILES

University of California, Berkeley

ACCORDING TO ESTABLISHED wisdom, the Scandinavian settlements in England left little imprint on the language of Anglo-Saxon literature even though English and Norse were long spoken side by side. As H. R. Loyn puts it, "Traditional literary Anglo-Saxon, affected by the conservatism of a mature written convention, shows (except in the legal field) comparatively little sign of this long linguistic symbiosis" (118).

Although sound in the main, this negative judgment may have to be modified in the light of recent studies. Fred C. Robinson has pointed out a cluster of Scandinavian locutions in the *Battle of Maldon* that appear to add up to "the first literary use of dialect in English" (26). Roberta Frank, in a 1981 article as well as in her essay in the present volume, has called attention to apparent skaldic influence on *Beowulf* and a striking skaldic configuration in *Exodus*, among other possible points of Norse influence on the poetry. Joseph Harris has called attention to some skaldic passages that throw light on a noted crux in verses 12b–13a of the *Battle of Brunanburh*.[1]

Following Harris in particular, I wish to suggest that the *Battle of Brunanburh* is best read within the context of an emerging tenth-century Anglo-Norse poetics. Given the haphazard nature of our literary records from the period before the Conquest, it is not clear that this poetics was ever much more than an inviting road not taken. Still, the existence of *Brunanburh* suggests that at least one Anglo-Saxon poet developed his language, verse technique, and authorial voice with some knowledge of Old Norse and some appreciation for the art of the skalds.

Though often grouped with *Maldon*, *Brunanburh* is clearly a poem of a different order. Unlike neighboring prose entries in the *Anglo-Saxon Chronicle*, the poem is not a summary of a military campaign but rather a panegyric composed on the occasion of the great English triumph of 937. More precisely, the author celebrates the victory that confirmed Athelstan's control of a combined Anglo-Danish kingdom, including Mercia and York, in the face of an invasion by an allied force consisting of the armies of Olaf Guthfrithson of Dublin, Constantine II of Scotland,

and (as we know from other sources) Owen of Strathclyde. The invaders' local allies doubtless included Hiberno-Norse settlers who during the preceding decades had established themselves from the Wirral peninsula to the Solway Firth.

Although most modern commentators have disclaimed knowledge of where Brunanburh is, or have guessed rather freely, there are reasons to conclude that the battle was fought at Bromborough, Cheshire, at the base of the Wirral (Dodgson 1953–57, following Smith). Twelfth- and thirteenth-century records reflect a regular linguistic development from Anglo-Saxon *Brunanburh* to the modern form of the name,[2] and Dodgson has pointed out that this site has historical plausibility. Other nominations for the site have recently been advanced by Alfred P. Smyth (41–55) and Michael Wood, but as R. I. Page suggests in a review article, they are based on airy webs of historical speculation. Philology alone cannot settle the matter. Even though the identification *Bromborough/Brunanburh* is impeccable, there is no way of knowing if this Brunanburh is *our* Brunanburh; hence the door to scholarly invention remains ajar.

The exact makeup of the English army is unclear. To judge from the number of Norse-named leaders who assembled at Winchester and Nottingham in 934, presumably to aid Athelstan's Scottish campaign of that year (Stenton 337–38, Birch nos. 702 and 703), the Mercian contingent probably included a significant number of Danes. There is nothing odd in this supposition, as the converted and anglicized Danes who by this time were firmly established east of the Pennines had more to gain from solidarity with their English overlord than from alliance with the Dublin-based Norsemen who were bent on checking Athelstan's power in the north.

Dobbie characterizes the *Battle of Brunanburh* as "an unrestrained song of triumph, in which the poet seems to know little, and care less, of the actual course of events, but gives full play to his feelings of exultation at the victory over a foreign foe" (xl). It is worth stressing, though, that this poem is far from a spontaneous outpouring of emotions. Few poems of the Anglo-Saxon corpus are as carefully crafted, verse by verse. Few are as self-consciously literary in their conception, from the first word *Her* 'Here', designating the numeral *dccccxxxvii* in the left-hand margin, to the concluding reference to what "bec, / ealde uðwitan," 68b–69a ("books, / ancient sages"), including the *Chronicle* itself, have to say about the first coming of the Angles and Saxons to Britain.[3] Campbell has pointed out how systematically the poet puts the conventional word-hoard of Anglo-Saxon poetry on display (38–40). Others have drawn attention to the poem's studied artistry, including its use of syntactic variation, studied antithesis, aural patterning, and an array of rhetorical figures that may be patterned on Latin models (Bolton, Johnson, Lawlor, Addison, Frese). The effect is, in Campbell's terms, "artificial" and "extremely careful," as if the author "had meticulously studied earlier

Old English verse" to create a text that would appeal to a courtly circle or to cultured monks (38).

And yet, by Old English standards, there is something unconventional about the poet's voice as well. Granted that the distribution of praise and blame is central to the purposes of early Germanic poetry, still nowhere else in Old English is there such a quintessential poem of boasting and scorn.[4] Athelstan's triumph is celebrated not by a sober account of his actions, but by exultant allusion to the enemy blood spilled on the field and the number of enemy kings and noblemen cut down. The poet's bloody-mindedness is matched by his emphasis on the losers' shame. The survivors take to their ships *æwiscmode* 'humiliated' (56b), while the victors proceed home *wiges hremge* 'gloating in battle' (59b). The satiric element that runs through the poem is most prominent in the threefold repetition "hreman ne þorfte. . .Gelpan ne þorfte. . .hlehhan ne þorftun," 39b, 44b, 47b ("he had no need to gloat. . .He had no need to boast. . .they had no need to laugh"). The poet here makes sardonic reference to the grief of the aged Scottish king Constantine, who not only lost his son on the battlefield but was unable to recover the young man's body.

The cruel note struck in this part of the poem is equally evident in the later passage that savors the image of the raven, eagle, and wolf feeding on the corpses of the unrecovered slain (60–65a). The motif of the birds and beasts of battle is of course a commonplace of both Old English and Old Norse poetry. In most other instances in Old English, however, the motif is introduced in anticipation of a battle. Usually it conveys an evenhanded horror, as the carrion creatures are imagined to feed on the slain of either side.[5] Here the only dead seem to be enemy dead. There are no regrets. The poet contemplates the fate of the corpses with the same grim equanimity with which he then takes pride in the body count: "Ne wearð wæl mare / on þis eiglande æfre gieta / folces gefylled beforan þissum," 65b–67 ("There was no greater slaughter / on this island ever yet / of a host cut down before this")—or at least there was no such bloodbath since the invading Angles and Saxons, *wlance wigsmiþas* 'proud warsmiths' (72a), first slaughtered the native Britons.

The poet's brusque indifference to carnage may remind one of the hard, cold tone that is characteristic of skaldic verse more than it calls to mind the heroic spirit of *Beowulf* or *Maldon*, let alone the melancholy and philosophical mood in which both the *Beowulf* poet and the poet of the *Wanderer* contemplate the spiraling tragedies of earthly mutability. If *Brunanburh* has affinities to other early medieval verse, they are to such a poem as the *Battle of Hafsfjord* rather than to anything in Old English, as Kershaw has pointed out (vii). Both these poems celebrate a decisive battle by which a king established authority over the whole of his realm. In the Norse poem the king is Harald Fairhair, and his opponents are a coalition of Norwegians who opposed his expanding power in 872.

Even more than the author of *Brunanburh*, the Norse poet takes delight
in the image of boats manned by fleeing survivors, who in this poem
are pelted with stones from behind while the wounded hunch shame-faced
under the rowing-benches:

> Slógusk und sesspiljur   es sárir váru,
> létu upp stöjlu stúpa,   stungu í kjöl höfdum [Kershaw 90].

> (They threw themselves under the seat-planks, those who
> were wounded, they stuck their rumps up in the air, they
> thrust their heads in the keel [Calder 141]).

In *Hafsfjord* as in *Brunanburh*, the poet follows the customary mode of
panegyric and calls attention to the distinguished ancestry of the victorious
party: "konungr enn kynstóri," 1.2 ("the king of noble lineage"). He also
alludes in conventional fashion to the din of battle: "ísörn dúðu," 2.4
("swords clashed"), "hlömmum vas á hlífum," 3.4 ("shields clanged together"). *Brunanburh* resembles nothing else so much as *Hafsfjord* drawn
out to a more substantial and dignified length by an author who had at
his command the full resources of Anglo-Saxon poetic speech and used
those resources to honor his English king.

In commenting on the "elliptical, allusive, non-narrative style" of
the six encomiastic poems that are embedded in the *Anglo-Saxon Chronicle*, Opland suggests that this group of poems emerged due to the influence
of the court poetry of the skalds (173). Leaving the other five *Chronicle*
poems aside, since (with the possible exception of the poem on the capture
of the Five Boroughs) they do not seem much like *Brunanburh* except
in being occasional pieces, there is reason to think that the *Brunanburh*
poet had at least passing acquaintance with the Norse language and skaldic
poetic models. Several of the points of influence have been reviewed by
Dietrich Hofmann (165–67); these consist of *cnear* 'warship' (35a) as a
loanword, *sceard* 'deprived' (40b) used in a manner suggestive of Old
Norse idiom, *guðhafoc* 'war-hawk' (64a) as a kenning for 'eagle', and—
with less certainty—*eorlas* (31a) in the Norse sense of 'jarls'. Other
points worth identifying are the following.

1. In Norse fashion, the poet refers to the vikings' homeland as
Iraland, 56a (*Yraland* CD), instead of either *Scotland* (or *Scotta land* or
Scotta ealand), which was the usual Old English term for Ireland, or
Hibernia, which was the term used regularly in Anglo-Latin and sometimes in Old English literary texts. Likewise he calls the vikings' chief
city *Difelin*, 55b (*Dyflen* B, *Dyflin* C, *Dyflig* D), from Old Norse *Dyflinn*.
The place-name *Iraland* seems to be formed by standard means from the
genitive plural of the tribal name that appears in Old Norse as *Írar* 'the
Irish', from Gaelic *Eriu* 'Eire'. In Old English before the time of Ælfric,
the Irish are regularly called *Scottas*, as in the *Chronicle* entry for the
year 891, which tells of the arrival in Wessex of three *Scottas* from
Hibernia (that is, three Irish monks). The term *Iraland* is not found in

English before *Brunanburh* except in the *Chronicle* entry for the year 918 (A text; 915 C and D texts) and in King Alfred's account of certain geographical information given by his Norwegian guest Ohthere (Old Norse Óttarr). Ohthere evidently referred to Eire by its Norse name *Írland*, and the West Saxon scribe followed suit (Sweet 19, Lund 21–22).[6] As for *Difelin*, if the Gaelic place-name *Dublind* had entered English directly, rather than through the intermediary of Old Norse, it would have done so in the unmutated form *Dublina* or some variant, which is what we find in eleventh- and twelfth-century Anglo-Latin (Campbell 115–16). Very likely the terms *Iraland* and *Difelin* are such recent borrowings that they reflect the poet's familiarity with Old Norse.

2. The poet uses the word *cnear* (35a), a borrowing from Old Norse *knǫrr*, not in the normal prose sense of 'cargo ship' but in the poetic sense of 'warship'. This is the first of three recorded instances of the word in English. The *knǫrr* was the ordinary transport and trading vessel of the vikings. This particular *cnear*, however, is the royal vessel of Anlaf (Olaf Guthfrithson), king of Dublin and leader of the viking army. Unless some comedy is intended, based on the incongruity of the king being forced to flee in a merchant vessel, the author is following the skaldic practice observed in *Hafsfjord* 1.3 of using the word to refer to viking longships, as he does again in 53b, *nægledcnearrum* 'with nailed ships'.

3. In a flamboyant display of the device of variation, the poet introduces three successive kennings that designate "battle" ironically in terms of peaceful social interchange. Leveled to the nominative case, these are *garmitting* 'spear-meeting' (50a), *gumena gemot* 'assembly of men' (50b), and *wæpengewrixl* 'weapon-exchange' (51a). The sardonic note in these kennings comes from the positive connotation of the second element. The usual purpose of a *gemot* or *mitting* is to resolve or forestall conflict; a *gewrixl* in its literal sense is an exchange of goods. The first two of these kennings seem to be formed by analogy with any number of skaldic battle-kennings based on the idea of an assembly of weapons, for example, *sverdþing* 'sword-meeting', *eggþing* 'edge-meeting', *geirþing* 'spear-meeting', *vápnþing* 'weapon-meeting', *brynþing* 'byrnie-meeting', and *malmþing* 'metal-meeting' (Jónsson s.v. *þing*). The third kenning may be an adaptation of Old Norse *vápnaskipti* 'exchange of weapons', hence 'fight'. The wordplay of this section of *Brunanburh* echoes the ironic term *hondplega* 'hand-to-hand play' that is introduced as a battle-kenning in 25b, but unlike this latter term, which is commonplace in Old English, the three kennings of 50a–51a are strikingly original. This is the only occurrence of *garmitting* in Old English. *Wæpengewrixl* occurs elsewhere only in Wulfstan's *Sermo Lupi ad Anglos*, where it again refers specifically to fighting between Englishmen and heathen Norsemen (Bethurum 263–64, 271). *Gumena gemot* is paralleled in verse 2b of the Old English *Descent into Hell* but there carries the literal sense of 'group of men'.

Only in the later (and Norse-influenced) poem of *Maldon* is the word *gemot* used metaphorically to denote 'battle' (301a), one hundred lines after it appears in the literal sense 'assembly' (199b).

4. A more striking Nordicism is the "skaldic" conceit that the poet introduces in 12b–13a: "Feld dænnede / secga swate" ("The field resounded / with the blood of men"). Many commentators and translators have shunned this meaning of *dænnede* (*dennade* BC, *dennode* D). Tupper found the verses "such an absurdity that we must seek some other meaning of the word" (93), and he and other scholars proceeded to do so. Some recent commentators, following Björkman and others before him, have rightly taken the form as a variant of the preterite singular of the common verb *dynian* 'resound', as in *Elene* 50b, *rand dynede* 'the shield rang', and *Judith* 204b, *dynedan scildas* 'shields resounded'. The scribe of British Library manuscript Cotton Otho B. xi, which was destroyed by fire in 1731, interpreted the line thus. When copying the A manuscript of the *Chronicle*, as Campbell has shown (134, 138, 141), he wrote *feld dynede*. The grounds that have been cited to justify this reading are not wholly persuasive, however. There is no synesthesia here, in the usual sense of that word, despite Robinson's claim to have found it (106–07), a claim that Greenfield and Calder accept (149). There is no shift of sensory perception whereby concurrent appeal is made to several senses, such as hearing in terms of smell or touch in terms of taste (Shipley 327, and see Bergman 103–04 for examples from modern poetry and speech). Rather, the poet is invoking the commonplace motif of the noise of weapons that cause blood to flow. Berkhout, while speaking of synesthesia but arguing for a literal reading of the lines, cites the scriptural passage in which God summons Cain: "Vox sanguinis fratris tui clamat ad me de terra," Genesis 4.10 ("The voice of your brother's blood calls out to me from the ground"). It is unclear, however, why an Anglo-Saxon poet celebrating the slaughter of Athelstan's enemies would wish to associate them with Cain's good brother. The visual image of blood crying out from the earth is wrong as well. In *Brunanburh* the blood has not seeped into the ground; rather, it is said to flow from reiterated wounds all day long from sunup to sundown.

The best way to interpret these verses and keep the manuscript reading, as Harris suggests, is to take "Feld dænnede / secga swate" as a boldly elliptical phrase of the kind favored by the skalds. The field resounded from the clash of weapons; the clash of weapons caused blood to flow. With a kind of wry skaldic shorthand, based on omission of the middle element in this series, the poet can therefore speak of the field as having resounded from the flow of blood. The clash of weapons is such an omnipresent feature of Old English and Old Norse battle poetry that the poet takes its presence for granted, just as his audience should do. In case there were any doubt, the verb *dynian* echoes skaldic battle-kennings like *sverddynr* 'sword-din', *hjǫrrdynr* 'blade-din', and *malmdynr* 'din of metal'. Later the poet calls specific attention to the sound of battle with the terms *bilgesleht* 'sword-clash' (45b) and *cumbolgehnast* 'standard-clash' (49b), so that the noise of iron smashing against iron is never far from the reader's consciousness. Although none of the skaldic parallels that Harris cites in support of this reading can bear much weight individually, the strategy of metaphor that is operative here is so typical of Old Norse court poetry in general (as this strategy is described, for example, by Hollander 13–14) that there is good reason to conclude that the English poet had Norse models in mind.

5. Possibly but not certainly, a second "skaldic" conceit may underlie the verses "þær læg secg mænig / garum ageted" (17b–18a). The sense here, usually taken to be "there lay many a man *destroyed* with spears" (Campbell 123, Toller s.v. *agitan*), may more precisely be "there lay many a man *bled to death* by spears." This reading depends on taking the verb *agetan* (or, in its various Anglo-Saxon spellings, *agitan, agietan, agytan*) as a weak secondary verb formed from the past participle *agoten* of the common strong verb *ageotan* 'pour out, shed' (cf. Kock 1). Since this latter verb is often used in the specific sense of 'shed blood,' the verb *agetan* seems originally to have meant 'cause (someone or something) to bleed', or 'bleed (someone or something) to death'. From this sense it takes on the general meaning 'kill' or 'destroy', which is the only meaning ascribed to it by Toller. If the *Brunanburh* poet is deliberately activating the root etymological sense of the verb, as I suggest he is, then the passage affords further evidence of both his fondness for wordplay and his taste for somewhat grotesque imagery.[7] The poet's prominent allusion to the flow of blood in the preceding verses (12b–17a) is capped by a wry phrase that specifies what the result of all this bloodshed is, namely a heap of corpses bled white.

If the preceding points have substance, there is something anomalous about the *Battle of Brunanburh* being taught in introductory Old English courses as a primary specimen of Anglo-Saxon poetry. *Brunanburh* is a showpiece of the Anglo-Saxon poetic style, true. It also is a development of a kind of encomiastic court poetry that came to maturity far from English shores before this anonymous tenth-century author tried his hand at it. Mingled with the poem's many borrowings from the language of Anglo-Saxon heroic poetry are several specific debts to the language and poetic techniques of the Norsemen. In addition, the poet views warfare from a coldly detached stance that is far from what we find in other Old English verse. There are no extravagant gestures of heroism here, no insights into human suffering. The seventy-three lines of the poem play out adept variations on a twofold theme: the glory of the victors and the humiliation of the vanquished. The judgment that Klaeber expressed in 1925 is still worth recalling:

> The author of the poem goes far beyond the legitimate patriotic zeal of the annalist in striking a strangely cruel note of bloodthirsty

violence. His way of lingering on the gruesome slaughter, the
revelling in the blood of battle, the absence of a true contest of
valor actually seem to suggest a foreign note [6].

The author of *Brunanburh* was a poet's poet, and a king's. However
much we may admire his achievement, it resists our emotional engage-
ment. In much the same way, the hard, compact, daring, and frequently
sardonic stanzas of the skalds ask for the audience's admiration and often
nothing else. We can be thankful for the existence of *Brunanburh* not
only because it is a brilliant piece of writing, but also because it hints
at the new directions for English poetry that ninth- and tenth-century
Scandinavian contacts were making possible. At the same time as the
poem dazzles us, it reminds us by contrast of the deep insights into
human loss and exultation that are offered by other Old English poems
that were not so much under the viking spell.

---

[1] My work on the present article was complete, I thought, when several readers drew
my attention to Harris's essay, thus saving me the embarrassment of trying to make a point
that he had already presented with characteristic thoroughness.

[2] The sequence of changes can be abstracted as follows. *Brunanburh* by loss of nasali-
zation after an unstressed vowel yields *Bruneburgh*, which by syncope of the unstressed
vowel gives *Brunburgh*. Assimilation of *n* to the following bilabial gives *Brumburgh*, and
lowering of the first *u* in anticipation of the following vowel, which had become lax in a
position of secondary stress, gives *Bromburgh*, or modern *Bromborough*. All these spellings
(together with numerous variations) are found in the historical records, not necessarily in
this sequence (Dodgson 1972, 237–38).

[3] Quotations of *Brunanburh* are from Dobbie, whose text is based on manuscript A of
the *Chronicle*, the Parker manuscript, with variant readings from manuscripts B, C, and
D. See Dobbie xxxiii-xxxiv for a description of the manuscripts.

[4] I take issue here with Lipp, who puts forth the unusual and, I think, too kind view
that the poet introduces a note of sympathy for the pains of the vanquished as "forceful
demonstrations of the perennial sufferings of man, caught in a moment of this transitory
life" (177). Unless many readers besides myself are mistaken, the English poet is delighted
that the heathen Norsemen and their rebellious Scottish allies got what they deserved.

[5] The theme is anticipatory in *Beowulf* 3024b–27, *Elene* 27b–30a and 110b–13a, *Exodus*
162–67, *Finnsburh* 5b–6a, *Genesis A* 1883b–85a, *Judith* 205b–12a, and *Maldon* 106–07.
In *Finnsburh* 34b–35a, *Genesis A* 2157b–61, and *Judith* 295–96a, the theme is raised for
a second time in each work in the context of a battle in progress or already won. Only in
the Biblical passages is the theme raised in a gloating tone, in satisfaction that the enemies
of the Jews get their just deserts. In *Beowulf*, as Bonjour has ably pointed out, the theme
enforces a mood of desolation at the prospect of a fate that awaits the speaker's own tribe,
so that "beyond the ominous dialogue of the beasts of battle there looms the shadow not
only of the death of warriors, but of the bondage and death of a glorious people" (569).

[6] The supposition, recently repeated by Fell (63), that Ohthere spoke of *Ísland* rather
than *Írland* and a West-Saxon scribe got it wrong, is improbable given that *Irland* (or
Iraland) was not a familiar English name at this time. The scribe of the A text of *Brunanburh*,
for example, seems to have been puzzled enough by the name that he substituted for it the
easier reading *hira land* 'their land'.

[7] The author's artistry was not appreciated by the scribe of the B manuscript, who
substituted for *ageted* the easier, but less apt, reading *forgrunden* 'ground to bits', thereby
playing an uninspired variation on 43b, *wundun forgrunden* 'ground to bits by wounds'.

WORKS CITED

Addison, James C., Jr. "Aural Interlace in 'The Battle of Brunanburh.'" *Language and Style* 15 (1982): 267–76.

Bergman, David and Daniel Mark Epstein. *The Heath Guide to Poetry*. Lexington, Mass.: Heath, 1983.

Berkhout, Karl T. "*Feld Dennade*—Again." *ELN* 11 (1974): 161–62.

Birch, Walter de Gray. *Cartularium Saxonicum*. 3 vols. London: Whiting, 1885–93.

Björkman, Erik. "Zum altenglischen Gedicht von der Schlacht bei Brunanburh." *Archiv für das Studium der neueren Sprachen und Literaturen* 118 (1907): 384–86.

Bolton, W. F. "'Variation' in *The Battle of Brunanburh*." *Review of English Studies* ns 19 (1968): 24–33.

Bonjour, Adrien. "*Beowulf* and the Beasts of Battle." *PMLA* 52 (1957): 563–73.

Calder, Daniel G. et al., eds. and trans. *Sources and Analogues of Old English Poetry II: The Major Germanic and Celtic Texts in Translation*. Cambridge: D. S. Brewer, 1983.

Campbell, Alistair, ed. *The Battle of Brunanburh*. London: Heinemann, 1938.

Dobbie, Elliott Van Kirk, ed. *The Anglo-Saxon Minor Poems*. Vol. 6 of *The Anglo-Saxon Poetic Records*. New York: Columbia University Press, 1942.

Dodgson, J. McN. "The Background of *Brunanburh*." *Saga-Book of the Viking Society* 14 (1953–57): 303–16.

———. *The Place-Names of Cheshire*. Part 4. English Place-Name Society 47. Cambridge: Cambridge University Press, 1972.

Greenfield, Stanley B. and Daniel G. Calder. *A New Critical History of Old English Literature*. New York: New York University Press, 1986.

Fell, Christine E. "Some Questions of Language." In Lund, 56–63.

Frank, Roberta. "Skaldic Verse and the Date of *Beowulf*." *The Dating of Beowulf*. Ed. Colin Chase. Toronto: University of Toronto Press, 1981. 123–39.

Frese, Dolores Warwick. "Poetic Prowess in *Brunanburh* and *Maldon*: Winning, Losing, and Literary Outcome." *Modes of Interpretation in Old English Literature: Essays in Honour of Stanley B. Greenfield*. Ed. Phyllis Rugg Brown et al. Toronto: University of Toronto Press, 1986. 83–99.

Harris, Joseph. "*Brunanburh* 12b–13a and Some Skaldic Passages." *Magister Regis: Studies in Honor of Robert Earl Kaske*. Ed. Arthur Groos et al. New York: Fordham University Press, 1986. 61–68.

Hofmann, Dietrich. *Nordisch-englische Lehnbeziehungen der Wikingerzeit*. Biblioteca Arnamagnæana 14. Copenhagen: Munksgaard, 1955.

Hollander, Lee M. *The Skalds: A Selection of Their Poems with Introduction and Notes*. Ann Arbor: University of Michigan Press, 1945.

Johnson, Ann S. "The Rhetoric of Brunanburh." *Philological Quarterly* 47 (1968): 487–93.

Jónsson, Finnur. *Lexicon poeticum antiquae linguae septentrionalis*. 2nd ed. Copenhagen: Møller, 1931.

Kershaw, N., ed. *Anglo-Saxon and Norse Poems*. Cambridge: Cambridge University Press, 1922.

Klaeber, Friedrich. "A Note on The Battle of Brunanburh." *Anglica: Untersuchungen zur englischen Philologie Alois Brandl*. Vol. 2. Leipzig: Mayer & Müller, 1925. 1–7. Issued as *Palaistra* 148 (1925): 1–7.

Kock, Ernst A. "Jubilee Jaunts and Jottings." *Lunds universitets årsskrift*, första afdelningen ns 14.2, no. 24 (1918): 1–82.

Lawlor, Traugott. "*Brunanburh*: Craft and Art." *Literary Studies: Essays in Memory of Francis A. Drumm*. Ed. John H. Dorenkamp. Wetteren, Belgium: Cultura Press, 1973. 52–67.

Lipp, Frances Randall. "Contrast and Point of View in *The Battle of Brunanburh*." *Philological Quarterly* 48 (1969): 166–77.

Loyn, H. R. *The Vikings in Britain*. London: Batsford, 1977.

Lund, Niels, ed. *Two Voyagers at the Court of King Alfred*. Trans. Christine E. Fell. York:

William Sessions, 1984.

Opland, Jeff. *Anglo-Saxon Oral Poetry: A Study of the Traditions*. New Haven: Yale University Press, 1980.

Page, R. I. "A Tale of Two Cities." *Peritia* 1 (1982): 335–51.

Robinson, Fred C. "Some Aspects of the *Maldon* Poet's Artistry." *Journal of English and Germanic Philology* 75 (1976): 25–40.

Shipley, Joseph T. *Dictionary of World Literary Terms*. 3rd ed. Boston: The Writer, Inc., 1970.

Smith, A. H. "The Site of the Battle of Brunanburh." *London Mediaeval Studies* 1 (1937–39): 56–59.

Smyth, Alfred P. *Scandinavian York and Dublin: The History and Archaeology of Two Related Viking Kingdoms*. Vol. 2. Dublin: Templekieran Press, 1979.

Toller, T. Northcote. *An Anglo-Saxon Dictionary: Supplement*. Oxford: Oxford University Press, 1921.

Tupper, Frederick, Jr. "Notes on Old English Poems." *Journal of English and Germanic Philology* 11 (1912): 82–103.

Wood, Michael. "Brunanburh Revisited." *Saga-Book of the Viking Society for Northern Research* 20 (1980): 200–17.

MALDON AS IT REALLY WAS

(Reconstructed From a Recently Discovered Eyewitness Report)

OLAF. (*with greedy gesticulation*): Afráð!

BYRHTNOÐ. Non intellego quod dicis, domine.[1]

OLAF. (*making repeated and vigorous gestures toward the rings on his arms*): Baugar, maðr, baugar!

BYRHTNOÐ. Baugar? Oh yes, beagas. Yes indeed, very nice rings indeed sir, very becoming.

OLAF. (*under his breath*): Damned Limey. (*Turning to his troops:*) Interpreter, front and center.[2] We'll spell it out for this half-wita. (*He dictates:*)

> Snjallir sæfarar   mik senda til þíns;
> þér segja hétu   senda snemma[3]
> bauga til bjargar;   ok betr væri
> gjalda afráð   fyrir geirvígi
> en harða hildi   heyja skyldim.
> Now, I want you to make that perfectly clear!

INTERPRETER. (*fidgets nervously with his runic notes and translates*):

> Me sendon to þe   sæmen snelle;
> heton ðe secgan   þæt þu most sendan raðe
> beagas wið gebeorge;   and eow betere is
> þæt ge þisne garræs   mid gafole forgyldon
> þonne we swa hearde   hilde dælon.

BYRHTNOÐ. Metrum agnoscens, verba tua libenter amplector, sed sensum eorum procul abjicio.[4]

OLAF. (*impatiently*): Ekki veit ek hvat maðrinn vill með þeiri svínalatínu. I'll give him one more chance. (*Addressing his lieutenant:*) Lieutenant, bring me the Old English phrasebook for tourists.

LIEUTENANT. (*Hands him the wrong book.*)[5]

OLAF. Not that one, blast you, not *Merry Old England on Five Øre a Day*. The other one, the phrasebook!

LIEUTENANT. (*Abashed, hands him the phrasebook.*)

OLAF. (*mumbling as he thumbs through the phrasebook*): "Blacksmiths and Armorers," "Monasteries with Accommodations for Tourists," "Bookings on Viking Ships," "Nightlife in the London Stews." (*Olaf pauses reflectively, then leafs ahead:*) Here it is: "Demands for Tribute from the Local Population."

OLAF. (*facing Byrhtnoð and reading haltingly from the phrasebook*): Hwæt. . .we Gar-Denas. . .gomban. . .willan.[6]

BYRHTNOÐ. (*finally loses his patience and exclaims indignantly with an appropriate gesture*): Canis culum in tuo naso![7]

OLAF. Hvat sagði hundrinn þinn?[8]

BYRHTNOÐ. In fide, non curo quod dicis. Habeo satis ego.

OLAF. (*with a sudden brainstorm, speaking in measured cadences*): Nú eru tveir kostir, at verjask með hrausti eða deyja með skǫmm.

BYRHTNOÐ. (*seizing the import if not the exact words*): Dulce et decorum est pro patria mori. (*Waxes elegiac:*)

> Ure æghwylc sceal   ende gebidan
> worolde lifes;   wyrce se þe mote
> domes ær deaþe.[9]

OLAF. (*aside to his lieutenant*): I knew that would get him. You can always count on the Old English to swallow that stuff about honor. Let's see if he'll fall for the Anglo-Saxon fair play pitch too.

LIEUTENANT. Crazy, boss. Err. . .I mean, very good sir, admiral, sir.

OLAF. (*turning to Byrhtnoð and speaking very slowly*): Eigi. . . kunnu. . .vér. . .yfirganga. . .þvíat. . .vatn. . .er. . .kalt.

BYRHTNOÐ. (*signals his troops to fall back, draws himself up to his full height of 5'2", and proclaims:*)

> Cumaþ ceorlas   ofer ceald wæter.
> God ana wat   gumena sælgifa
> hwa þære wælstowe   wealdan mote.
> Ne wendaþ na   æt þam wigplegan
> þa hwile ðe we wæpna   wealdan moten.
> For life ne murnaþ. . . .

(*Before he can finish, the vikings charge across the inlet and wipe out the English in mid-sentence.*)

---

[1] Byrhtnoð replies in Latin. It is well known that the Anglo-Saxons enjoyed a more advanced culture than their rapacious neighbors. Byrhtnoð fails to understand the barbarous tongue from across the North Sea and replies in what he considers to be the standard of polite intercourse.

[2] That the Norsemen were frequently accompanied by interpreters on their cruises in foreign waters is indicated by a passage in *Orkneyinga saga* (ch. 85).

[3] Note that in his irritation Olaf commits a serious metrical blunder (alliteration in the fourth stress).

[4] Byrhtnoð shows an impressive command of patristic literature by paraphrasing Victor of Capua's preface to Tatian's Gospel Harmony.

⁵ Illiteracy was widespread among the ancient Norsemen, especially in the rank and file, and the lieutenant is probably unable to read the titles on the books.

⁶ The phrasebook was clearly compiled by someone familiar with eighth-century epic. We may surmise that it was composed in such a way as to impress the native with the user's culture, a sophisticated concept for such an early stage in the history of the phrasebook.

⁷ Byrhtnoð subtly implies that he, too, is well versed in the medieval phrasebook. See the so-called "Pariser Gespräche," ed. W. Braune, in the *Althochdeutsches Lesebuch* (Tübingen, 1952), p. 10. The response anticipates an episode at Bastogne a millenium or so later.

⁸ hundr = κύων (a term of abuse).

⁹ Another brilliant display of Byrhtnoð's knowledge of both older and more recent classics.

www.ingramcontent.com/pod-product-compliance
Lightning Source LLC
Chambersburg PA
CBHW030654110726
47901CB00002B/718